WORLD ARCHITECTURE TODAY

STAIRCASE, LEICESTER ENGINEERING FACULTY ▶
Archs: Stirling and Gowan
Photo: John Donat

WORLD ARCHITECTURE TODAY

EDITOR JOHN DONAT

A STUDIO BOOK · THE VIKING PRESS · NEW YORK

PYRAMIDAL KINDERGARTEN
LOURENÇO MARQUES
Arch: Guedes

Designed by
GILLIAN GREENWOOD
JOHN DONAT

Published in 1964 by The Viking Press, Inc.
625 Madison Avenue, New York, N.Y. 10022
Library of Congress catalog card number 64-11432
Printed in Great Britain by
Robert MacLehose & Company Limited, Glasgow

CONTRIBUTING EDITORS PANEL

ARGENTINA
J. J. Solsona

BRAZIL
David Crease*

CANADA
Anthony Jackson*

CHILE
Carlos Huidobro

CUBA
Rene Calvache

FINLAND
Esko Lehesmaa*

FRANCE
Shadrach Woods*

GERMANY
Erhard Duwenhogger*

GREAT BRITAIN
John Donat*

GREECE
Orestis Doumanis*

HUNGARY
Charles Polónyi*

INDIA
K. V. Satyamurti

ISRAEL
Ram Karmi*

ITALY
Maria Bottero*

JAPAN
Noriaki Kurokawa*

MEXICO
Eduardo Terrazas*

MOZAMBIQUE
Amancio Guedes*

NETHERLANDS
Aldo van Eyck
Herman Hertzberger*

NORWAY
John Lloyd*

POLAND
Jerzy Soltan
Oskar Hansen*

PORTUGAL
Luiz Cunha*

SPAIN
David Mackay*

SWEDEN
Office of Ralph Erskine*

SWITZERLAND
Bernhard Hoesli*

U.S.A. (EAST)
Kallman and McKinnell*

U.S.A. (WEST)
Patrick Morreau*

U.S.A. (MIDWEST)
Robertson Ward*
Louis Rocah*

VENEZUELA
Magali Ruz Brewer*
Oscar Tenreiro*

* Contributors to this volume

CONTENTS

Introduction

Good modern architecture is a rare bird. It takes interest, patience, and knowledge to track down. Even when we find it we are not sure what to think, what to say, what the architect is getting at, what it has to do with *us*. Everywhere the deadliness and mediocrity of our choked cities witness our failure to create an environment worth living in. Punch-drunk with the ugliness of our surroundings, we are forced to turn a blind eye because to see is to suffer. Commerce is the piper that calls the tune — most of us are deafened by the blast and frightened away from making any kind of value judgement.

Architecture, taken in its widest sense, should contribute to making a world worth living in and should affect us all deeply and personally — *we are involved*. But the architects are isolated from people, partly through their own esotericism (complete with high priests) but largely through the public's own lack of interest. This isolation of the architect from the society he is building for robs modern architecture of a shot in the arm it desperately needs: informed and outspoken lay criticism. Over the past few years there has been a noticeable quickening of interest, architecture has been brought more and more into the public eye. Even so, lay and press judgements are still based on a foundation of ignorance about what architects do, think, and feel, and the nature of the problems they attempt to solve.

The failure of communication between the architect and the public and the absence of critical criteria in lay and press judgements convinced us of the need for a periodic international review with a critical backbone, to present really good building in a way that will appeal as much to the awakening interest of the intelligent layman as to the specialist.

World Architecture, then, is an attempt to bridge the gap between architects and people, to show not only what architects are doing but what they are thinking, feeling, and concerned about. It is essentially non-technical and critical, not documentary. Nor has any attempt been made to present a unanimous or dogmatic point of view. A team of young contributing editors in nearly thirty countries has been given a completely free hand to select material and to write a vigorous commentary, supported wherever possible by personal statements from the architects themselves. Their selection has been based on those developments which seem most relevant in their own context at the present time; the emphasis is on new ideas, new directions, new thinking.

The variety that results reveals the contradictions as well as the vitality of an art trying to relate itself to a scientific and industrial world, its successes and its failures. Many of the buildings will be familiar; there is no attempt at novelty for its own sake. The highly personal work of the established masters is confronted with the vitality and energy of those less well known and younger architects whose influence is already being felt. As one contributor has written: 'Architecture is no longer the privilege of old and sacred cows — the small fry are swimming faster than the big fish — but we are all, still, much too cool.'

For the most part the examples chosen are isolated buildings — underlining our failure to think big enough to create a total environment — the 'mad jewellers' acts' that are a pitiful drop in the world building-ocean. But running through the book, like a tenuous thread, is the primary consideration facing architects today: the need to house the Greater Number. The world population explosion and the appalling division between the haves and have-nots demand that means should be found of housing millions of people without sacrificing that essential sense of identity and *place* that human habitation must possess. In these examples can be seen practical attempts to deal with the massive world problem of shelter, growth, and mobility which makes so much else that is being done seem pathetically misdirected. Perhaps the next few decades will narrow the gap between those thousands who are lucky to find shelter under a piece of corrugated iron and the lucky few who enjoy the sophisticated aesthetic exercises in the perfection of pure form which is the architects' obsession.

So much is written about technology and industrialization that it tends to obscure the fact that we have hardly improved on the Crystal Palace; our whole attitude to technology is still rooted in the nineteenth century. Certainly the building industry has not caught up with Henry Ford. Many architects are even turning their backs on the few advances that have been made, seemingly in despair of creating spaces with warmth and human associations out of the coldness and hardness of glass and steel. They have retreated into the comforting womb-like security of massive structures designed for twentieth-century cavemen in an atmosphere of earthy nostalgia. These architect-ostriches cannot hide from the future for long; it is their unquestioned creative imagination that must go hand in hand with advanced technical competence if we are to tame the machine and exploit its potentialities to create a true art-science that will transform our urban wastes into human places, our fragmented chaos into a total architecture.

John Donat

JAPAN

Contributing Editor

Noriaki Kurokawa

METABOLISM GROUP
Ikebukuro, a sub-centre
of Metropolitan Tokyo 1962

Metabolism: The Pursuit of Open Form

Architecture in Japan since the war can be divided into four groups according to different streams of influence, as follows:

1 Academic architecture — pseudo-functionalism behind a superficial mask of modern architecture — which is generally supported by officialdom and commercialism and has a tendency to hide its contradictions behind the ambiguity of its conception. It has a rather modern and rather moderate nuance.

2 Architecture strongly influenced by the expressionism of Le Corbusier, designed by architects such as Maekawa, Sakakura and Yoshizaka who have worked in Le Corbusier's atelier. Because construction employing reinforced concrete is so suitable to our country, buildings in this manner have strongly influenced a number of young Japanese architects.

3 Architecture influenced by Frank Lloyd Wright and northern European countries, which is designed by a few of the followers of Wright himself, such as Raymond, Endo and Amano. Belonging to this group also are a number of architects who aim to create 'free space' under the influence of northern European countries, but they are less influential than the architects influenced by Le Corbusier.

4 Traditional architecture — aiming to continue the expressionism of traditional Japanese architecture — represented by the buildings of Yoshimura, Yoshida and Taniguchi. Their architecture is deeply influenced by the traditional techniques and expression of wooden houses in Japan.

In a broad sense it may be said that each of these four groups belongs to a kind of 'expressionism'. It is now becoming evident that young Japanese architects and critics are reacting against the ideas of these groups, emphasizing the importance of re-establishing tradition to create a new philosophy.

The New Movement in Japanese Architecture

The new movement was born as a result of the World Design Conference in Tokyo, 1960, led by the Metabolism Group which includes architects, critics, graphic designers, city planners, painters and photographers.
The basis of Metabolism Group thinking is that they see architecture and city as a process of movement, change and development. In other words they conceive architecture and city as 'open form', not as 'closed form'.

The Moss Temple in Kyoto is one example of the traditional use of space in Japanese architecture. This Temple is recognized as one of the great masterpieces of architecture, even though changes have taken place and the trees have been replanted through generation after generation. The Shoin of Nijoji in Kyoto has a metabolic system in which tension and dynamic balance in the whole sequence of spaces exist at every stage in its growth. The Ise Shrine also exemplifies the traditional use of space in Japan and remains today in spite of being completely rebuilt again and again.

I believe that as a basic principle of architecture today we must pursue spatial 'archetype' and 'prototype', with which we can create dynamic space according to the inevitably changing needs of a constantly shifting society. In the illustrations that follow I have tried to present architecture based on a system which illuminates the meaning of 'archetype' and 'prototype'.

The Sky House by Kikutake is one of the results of his study of space where movable equipment is the keynote.

The Kurashiki City Hall by Tange evolves a 'major structure' and a 'minor structure', and the keynote is the potential changing of space within the 'major structure'.

In my own Labour Centre at Kyoto I have tried to establish the basis of a system which will influence the growth of this area in future, by introducing a 'passage system' into the area of tradesmen's houses in the old city of Kyoto.

Although other architects have published projects accepting space as a changing condition, I have shown the Kurashiki City Hall, the Sky House and the Labour Centre because they, I think, represent the new movement growing in Japanese architecture.

Noriaki Kurokawa

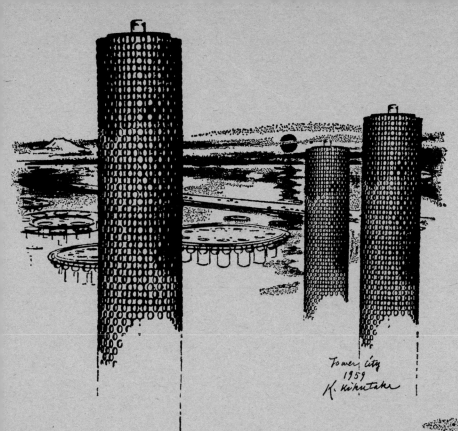

Tower City
1959
K. Kikutake

METABOLISM GROUP
The Tower City 1959

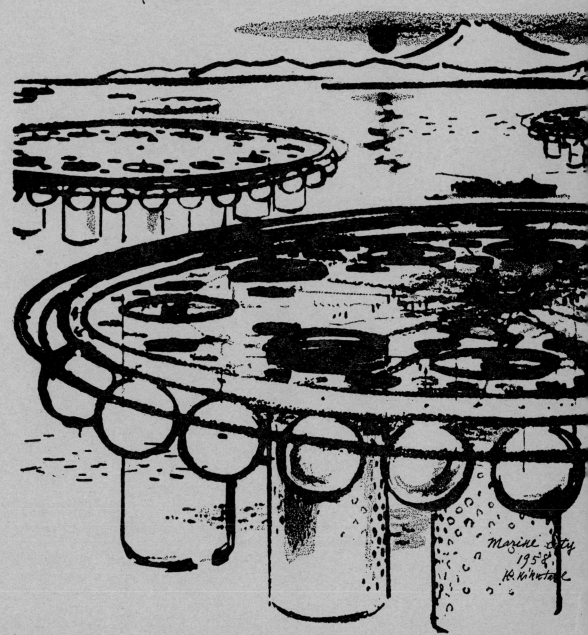

Marine City
1958
K. Kikutake

METABOLISM GROUP
The Marine City 1958

KURASHIKI CITY HALL

Architect

Kenzo Tange

The funds available for the city hall were by no means excessive, and pre-cast concrete and stainless steel were used wherever possible. The designers concentrated not so much on the technical aspects of the structure as on the nature of the building as part of an urban core, and on the technical means of creating a sense of spaciousness as well as a natural flow of space, from the plaza to the public hall and then to the counter section on the second floor. In the counter section, which is where public and official-dom actually meet, an attempt was made, on the one hand, to create an atmosphere of approachability and, on the other, to provide flexible spaces. The plan, consequently, is simple, as is that of the structure as a whole. Pre-cast concrete curtain walls were used for the entire exterior.

I believe we Japanese architects have considered Japanese tradition from almost every possible angle. The conclusion I have reached is that tradition is like a *catalyst* — it can stimulate or hasten creative activity, but not a trace of it should remain in the finished product. The white plaster walls and the beautiful tradition of Kurashiki were an inspiration to me and my team, but we made every effort to avoid any trace of them in our building.

In the case of Kurashiki, a general plan for the street system had been drawn up by two city-planners, and in connection with this a site had been set aside for the city hall and public auditorium. The decision as to the axis of the rectangular building was left to us, however, and we considered the matter very carefully before making up our minds, since this axis is the line around which the new Kurashiki will grow. I strongly hope that this city hall and auditorium will stimulate the redevelopment of Kurashiki.

The city hall faces a citizen's square that is soon to be completed, and the installation as a whole was designed to have what I call a 'mass-human' scale. In my opinion, this scale is manifested by the structure of the building. From the point of view of time, individual buildings are composed of a number of elements; some change in short cycles, others in long ones. Those that have long cycles are the ones that determine its character. With that in mind I chose a structure of steel and concrete, which stresses the fact that this is a contemporary building. Other materials — those which have been commercialized and which, under the name of 'factory-produced materials', are changing in shorter and shorter cycles — become dated, because each year's model is different, but they do not give the building the stamp of its period.

The mass-human scale is shown by a structure that has a long-term cycle. We first considered possibilities for the major structure, which determines the system of the whole building. Taking as basic two structural cores which enclose the central facilities and the vertical lines of traffic, we added to this a structure with a span of 20 metres. The long span was determined in part by the demand for interior space.

It was, however, no simple matter to associate this scale with the level of individual human scale. Consequently, we thought of a minor structure of precast concrete block and, after many trials, composed a single form and space. I regret that we were unable here to develop the full structural meaning of this minor structure. If also it does not satisfy the full requirements of human scale, it is because we wished, by establishing an order of scale sequences, to consider the organization of spatial flow from the plaza to the city hall and into the interior and, in a large sense, the hierarchy of urban space; that is to say of the space including the city hall, the plaza, and the surrounding houses.

Kenzo Tange

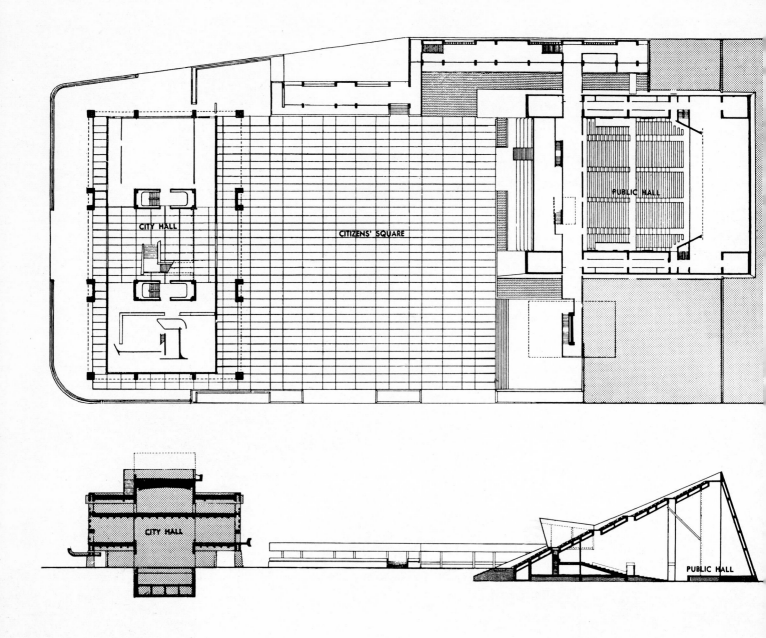

Kurashiki City is a local city in the western part of Japan, with long and venerable traditions. In this work Tange seems to expect a new birth of tradition by putting a space with entirely new scale and quality near old houses with white plaster walls and tile roofs. Tradition, here, acts just as a *catalyst*.

The problem which he proposes is how to integrate the urban scale, space and structure, and the human scale, space and structure. Though it could hardly be said that the conquest of large-span and the introduction of pre-cast units in this work are completely successful, a clue to 'open form' can be found in that the space of architecture and city possesses an element which changes in a long-cycle and another which changes in a short-cycle.

It is particularly interesting that Tange is continuing this line of thought in his work with the students of M.I.T. and in his other recent projects.

Noriaki Kurokawa

Above Plan and section showing the relationship between the City Hall, the proposed Public Hall and Citizens' Square.
Right Elevation of massive in-situ concrete frame detailing, with pre-cast concrete curtain wall elements aggressively reflecting the Japanese tradition of timber construction

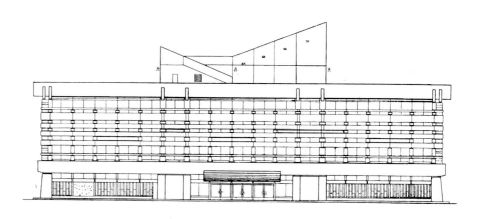

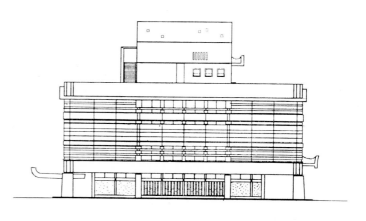

SKY HOUSE

Architect

Kinoryu Kikutake

To my thinking, architecture has three aspects: life, human space, and function.
Human space is by no means restricted merely to artificially created spaces. Further-more, it continues to exist even when it is not in use. The task of the creative architect is to discover new artificial forms of human space and to add them to the pre-existing human space. His task is to create space for the human in the dwelling and space for society in the city. Modern life demands a synthesis of this human space and of contemporary functions. The synthetic method has thus taken on a great importance. I use the term 'type' in characterizing this synthetic method.
I conceived the 'type' of this Sky House as being a human space consisting of a synthesis of square units around which movable units are grouped. This arrangement gives freedom from constraint to the living patterns found in the traditional Japanese way of life. Another concept to which I give assent is that the type of the contemporary dwelling is one in which man lives in the centre of the dwelling.
The bathroom, the kitchen, the lavatory, and the children's room are considered as functional, and their functions are performed by means of compact and efficient movable units. The movable units are constantly being modified and changed with changes in living patterns and with advances in technology. They ought to be capable of positive progress and of being replaced as needed. This is the direction in which I believe the dwelling of the future should progress. It is a dwelling subject to metabolic changes, and its ceaselessly changing appearance is precisely the moving 'form' of contemporary architecture.
The mutual interrelations of these freely changing and changeable 'forms' is what I call 'order'. The city must possess 'order'. Today it is our essential task to envisage an 'order' suitable to the present age, and to create appropriate 'types' and 'forms'.

Kinoryu Kikutake

The site is within the loop marking out the central part of metropolitan Tokyo. This area is the centre of the city and has an exceptionally large number of educational institutions; thus it is highly desirable as a living environment.
The building stands half way up a raised promontory and has a total lot area of 300 square metres. Since it is surrounded on all sides by wooden buildings, it was neces-sary to conceive it as a fireproof building of reinforced concrete.
As a solution to the problem of earthquakes in Japan, a special construction was adopted with a light shell roof, and wall columns. The total area of the two-storey building was 162 square metres. Additions can be made, such as the children's room now hanging from the second floor, and this gives it the nickname 'kangaroo house'.
The external finish consists of asphalt water-proof roofing and rough concrete. The inside has a white asbestos spray ceiling. The perimeter consists of three planes: the outer being a system of storm shutters which slide behind the wall-pillars in the day-time; the inner consisting of steel-sashed plate glass panels with sliding paper screens (shōji) on the interior.
The living patterns are planned according to the movable unit system. The facilities can be moved and replaced in accordance with the living requirements, and the furniture is arranged to suit the needs of any particular time within the one-room system. The living patterns can be modified according to the season of the year or the requirements of the time.

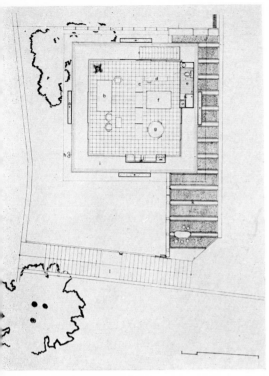

GROUND FLOOR PLAN

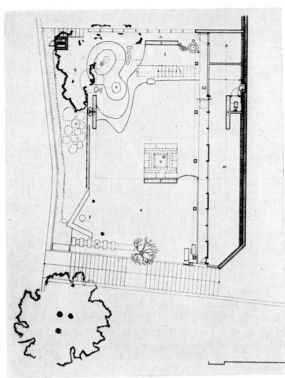

FIRST FLOOR PLAN

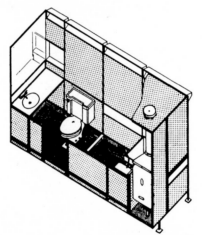

Bathroom and kitchen
self-contained movable units

The Sky House is also called the 'House of Light'. Great emphasis is laid on the variations and the adjustability of light.

Sunset is the most attractive type of sunlight. Its brightness and abundant colouring depend on its angle, as well as on its delicate changes and the speed with which these changes take place. For this reason, the Sky House does not face towards the south, which is the usual direction but, instead, towards the south-west.

The dwelling must be open and must have only one room in order to admit enough light. However, the control of light is particularly important.

Light is controlled in three different stages: the storm shutters made of a traditional louvre; the space of the surrounding passageway; and finally, the shōji on the inside of the glass doors.

The light of the sunset is replaced after nightfall by touching a button to give the artificial lighting used at night. The combination of indirect lighting by means of fluorescent lamps illuminating the floor surface and by movable paper lanterns gives a strong emphasis and support to family living. Thus 'living space' is created by light, and the living space is also vivified by light.

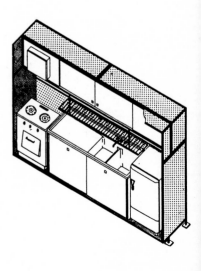

Photo: Kawasumi

Outer passageway lighting control zone. Storm shutters are stored between the handrail and the concrete column

Right Looking down at the guest room and study space

Family space: *right*, movable storage unit divides space

Photo: Futagawa

Photo: Futagawa

Storm shutters used for light control after sunset

Photo: Kawasumi

Photo: Kawasumi

Interiors showing sliding paper screens, kitchen movable unit (*extreme right*) and family space at night (*below*)

Photo: Futagawa

Photo: Futagawa   *Photo: Futagawa*   *Photo: Toshio Taira*

LABOUR CENTRE, NISHIJIN

Architect

Noriaki Kurokawa

Kyoto has the appearance of a lattice-work of streets and passages. 'Street' is a term used to indicate comparatively wide thoroughfares, which function both as arteries for traffic and as dividers for districts and areas. Opposed to these are 'passages', which have the characteristics of private space for the inhabitants, and are part of the architectural space of the buildings fronting on them; as continuations of the surrounding structures, they provide an atmosphere of privacy. Usually retailers and wholesalers in the same line of business are found grouped together on these 'passages', reinforcing the feeling of private group ownership. The wider streets are more public in nature and provide space for society in general. They are for everyone, like the public squares in Europe, and serve as outlets for the 'passages'.

Kyoto is a skilful composition of the interlacing 'streets' and 'passages', and it is in this old concept that we found the answer to our problem in designing the Nishijin Labour Centre.

Our problem was two-fold — human and architectural. The centre was built with funds contributed by foreign and Japanese Christian organizations and the city of Kyoto for the erection of medical and recreational facilities for the labourers of the Nishijin district. The building site was on a narrow street, Seiganji-dori, with heavy traffic and no parking permitted. We attempted to revive the old 'passage' atmosphere, which was lost when the general public began to use it, by retaining the old Kyoto-type wall along one side and designing the lower wing of the building along the other side to harmonize with the traditional architecture of the surrounding buildings. A parking area was built, and a small stream, in which a small Buddhist statue will later be placed, was incorporated into the plans. The area between the wall and the lower wing is the 'passage' or approach to the stairs of the main building, which can be thought of as a vertical continuation of the 'passage'.

Future plans are to extend the 'passage' through to the street at the back of the building.

Noriaki Kurokawa

PROJECT FOR GROWTH
The Labour Centre establishes
a new communication network for
roads, car parking, pedestrian
movement and open space that
could be extended throughout
Nishijin.

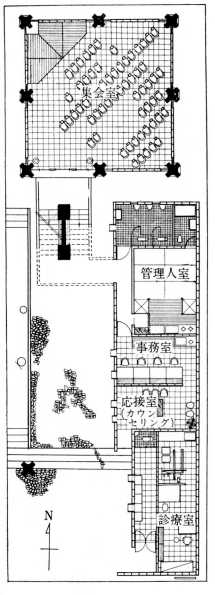
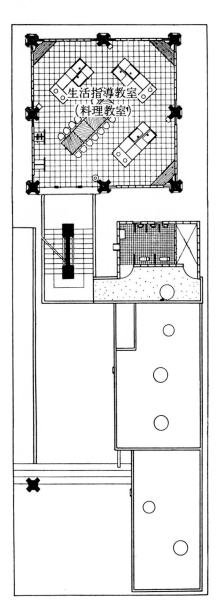
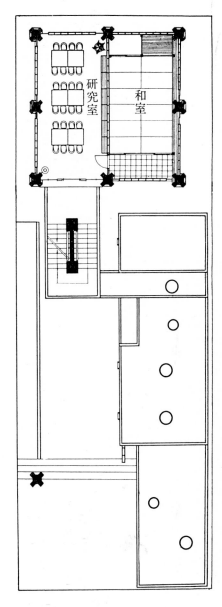

Ground floor plan   First floor plan   Second floor plan

Elevation   Section

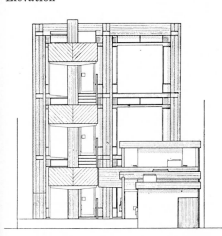

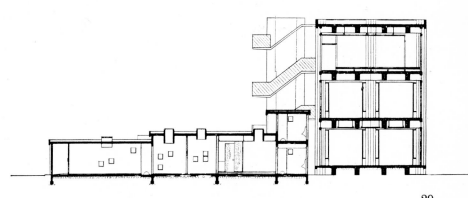

Photos: Futagawa

Left Entrance past water.

Right Balcony landings to concrete cantilevered staircases, balustrade clad in rough timber diagonal boarding.

Below Communal room planned on the diagonal established by the concrete frame dia-grid structure.

PRE-FABRICATED APARTMENTS

Photos: Watanabe

Architect

Noriaki Kurokawa

Quick, cheap and flexible industrial housing systems are a world need. In spite of significant developments of technique in Europe and Scandinavia, few systems give us any confidence in their ability to create a worthwhile living environment. Technically brilliant, sterile, egg-crate, people-packages laid out with ruthless formality in aseptic parallel blocks, are all too familiar.

In this project for high-density, low-cost, pre-fabricated apartments in Japan, Kurokawa has designed a system that rejects a rigid, repetitive cell-structure in favour of a free-form arrangement of structural and functional components that can be combined in a variety of ways. The result is tough and uncompromising, but it goes some way towards creating the kind of place one would like to be in and around.

The all-dry construction of pre-cast concrete elements is based on a modular system that carries right through to the design of built-in furniture units, leaving the maximum free living space. Pre-formed and completely equipped kitchens and bathrooms of moulded plastic slot into the framework with the ease and simplicity of a clip-on bow tie. Their location in the structure can be varied to suit a variety of plan types which are based on traditional mat sizes. As in other Metabolism Group thinking, tradition is *catalyst*. Groups of apartments can be built up in a linear form varying in height from two to four storeys, each group separated by access stairs on a split-level system. These staircases can be placed in varying positions according to individual flat plans, and create points of articulation where one block joins another allowing the linear form to be subtly staggered on plan.

The open-form staircases, slot-in bathrooms and kitchens, and clip-on pre-cast balconies complement the regular structural rhythm to create a convincingly consistent language of form; rich, vigorous and confident.

John Donat

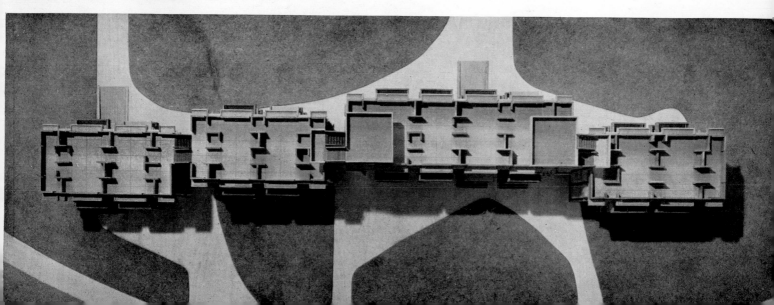

U.S.A.

Contributing Editors

East

G. Kallman

N. M. McKinnell

Middle West

Robertson Ward

Louis Rocah

West

Patrick Morreau

MEDICAL RESEARCH LABORATORIES, PHILADELPHIA

Architect

Louis Kahn

My medical research building at the University of Pennsylvania incorporates this realization that science laboratories are essentially studios, and that the air to be breathed must be separated from stale, waste air. The normal plan for laboratories places the work areas along one side of a central corridor, the other side of which houses the stairs, elevators, animal quarters, ducts and other facilities. In such a corridor there is mixed, together with the air you breathe, the outflow of contaminated, dangerous air. The only distinction between one man's work space and that of another is the difference in numbers on their doors. For the University, I designed three studio towers in which each man may work in his own bailiwick. Each studio in these towers has its own escape sub-tower and exhaust sub-tower for the release of isotope air, germ-infected air and noxious gases. A central building, around which the three major towers cluster, serves as the area for facilities, usually to be found on the opposite side of the corridor in the normal plan. This central building has nostrils for the intake of fresh air, located far from the exhaust sub-towers for vitiated air. This design, the result of consideration of the unique uses to be made of its spaces and their service requirements, expresses the character of the research laboratory. From what I have said I do not mean to imply a system of thought and work leading to realization from form to design. Design could just as well lead to realizations in form. This interplay is the constant excitement of architecture.

I do not like ducts; I do not like pipes. I hate them really thoroughly, but because I hate them so thoroughly, I feel that they have to be given their place. If I just hated them and took no care, I think they would invade the building and completely destroy it. I want to correct any notion you may have that I am in love with that kind of thing.

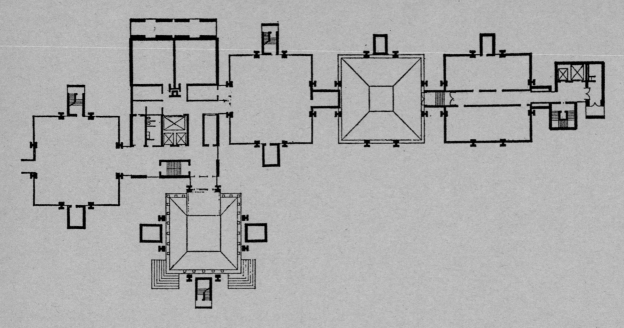

GROUND FLOOR PLAN

One day, waiting for a friend, I watched the crane lifting heavy members at the Medical Building at the University. On previous days watching its movement I resented its presence, a red painted monster, out of scale with the building and the members it was lifting into place; it imposed its image on every progress photograph. But because I had to hang around, it gave me a chance to reflect on its meaning, and I realized that the design of a building could have a direct bearing on how capable the crane is. I thought of columns a few hundred feet away from each other, carrying great spans. No longer did they appear as columns really but as stations, a composite grouping of service rooms composed of large prefabricated and intricate parts joining dramatically to each other. Truly, the joints of each fabricated part became strong and visible from a distance. This reminded me that joint is the beginning of ornament. Now the column formed a space, itself designed to serve the greater space. Because the members were so big, weighing even more than the crane before could carry, I imagined that I would demand bigger cranes and forget resentment. Now the joints waited to be emphasized with insertions of sculptured gold accents. The levels within the column were covered with marble. The members forming the sinews for its strength were carefully articulated to express its work. Small pieces coming together could not give rise to such thoughts . . . suddenly the crane became a friend.

Photo: Marshall D. Myer

Then I thought of the enclosure. Structures of old combined the roof and the wall with the same material. Now the column and the beam has become so capable through the science of concrete and steel that there is no rhythmic relationship to the enclosure. The enclosure, therefore, is on its own. It is even conceivable that one could build a stone building in the Renaissance manner to encircle the structure. This building could contain the rooms needed to serve the great interior. If we think in terms of the materials of today, then it is enclosed in a curtain of glass. And to emphasize the miracle of glass, the mullions would also be of glass. I did not want to accept the enormous tenacity of steel in so minor a role as to divide one piece of glass from another. When I thought it over, however, I realized the whole thing was pretty flimsy, but then a thin, little man with a high voice said to me 'You need help. May I introduce myself. I am Mr Stainless Steel. I can teach you how to reinforce glass and glass mullions with these miracle strands, using them only where they can brace the glass without shading their powers'. Now I learned another lesson, that each material has its design position in architecture. So I reflected on the crane and its influence, in thoughts about design.

Louis Kahn

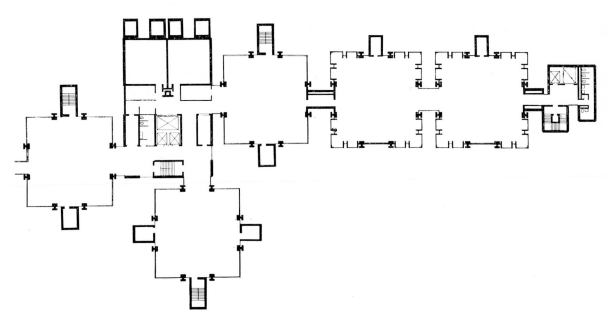

TYPICAL FLOOR PLAN

Photos: Malcolm Smith

ARTS CENTRE, HARVARD

Architect

Le Corbusier

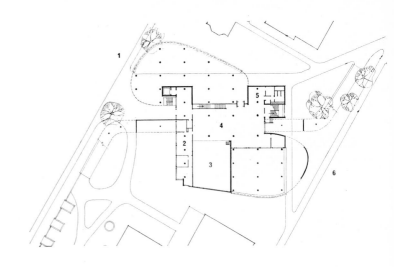

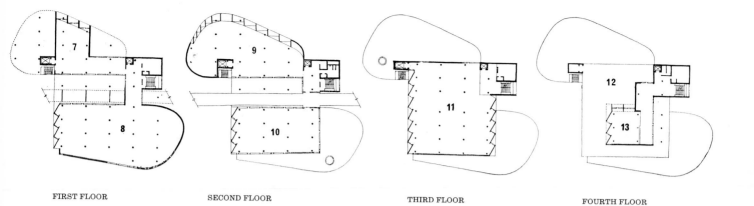

FIRST FLOOR   SECOND FLOOR   THIRD FLOOR   FOURTH FLOOR

KEY
1 Prescott Street
2 Administration
3 Lecture Room
4 Common Room
5 Lobby
6 Quincy Street
7 Director's Studio
8 Studio space
9 Studio space
10 Exhibition space
11 Exhibition space
12 Roof Garden
13 Visitor's Studio

Above: Ramp from Prescott Street
Below: Ramp from Quincy Street

The Carpenter Center for the Visual Arts provides teaching space for a variety of disciplines; fine arts, art history, photography, psychology and perception, urban design, two- and three-dimensional design, with a rooftop studio for a resident artist. The judgement on Hamlet (so full of quotations) might well be passed on Corbusier's first building in the United States. With deceptive casualness he quotes from the familiar vocabulary of his own past work. The sweeping movement of pedestrian ramps up to the entrances in the heart of the building refer back originally to Poissy. The interplay of spaces from level to level has been a consistent theme throughout his work since the villa at Garches. The 'free space' in a forest of columns dates from his early thoughts about the liberation of the wall through frame structures. The light-controlling screen walls, brise soleils, vertical 'aerateurs', irregular window mullions, glass bricks and vivid primary colours each refer to their origins in Rio, Ahmedabad, La Tourette, La Cité de Réfuge, and Marseille.
All are dressed in the roughest country tweed of raw concrete, in emphatic contrast to their urbanely well dressed neo-Georgian neighbours. (Do the construction photographs also show the donkeys? The women carrying mortar on their heads? Whither technology?) (continued)

It may be unfair to present the Arts Centre as a whimsical collage from the Oeuvre Complète; certainly all the familiar elements are brought together with the decision and relaxed authority expected of the master of light and form, who creates his own rough poetry out of people and space. It is a building to arouse fierce emotions; it will be loved and hated. Its apparent lack of sympathy for the local environment can also be seen as a stinging comment on the state of contemporary architectural thinking in America. Harvard has added an aggressively eloquent work of art to its collection.

Above: Exterior from Quincy Street

Centre: Two-dimensional studio

Below: Three-dimensional studio

UNITED AIRLINES OFFICES, CHICAGO

Architects

Skidmore, Owings and Merrill

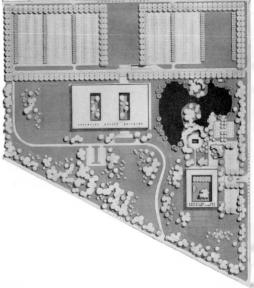

This is an example of the current trend towards office decentralization in the United States. The executive offices are built on a semi-rural, fifty-one acre site, north-west of Des Plaines, Illinois. Design criteria for the utmost flexibility of interior space determined the structural solution of large bay sizes combined with interior courts and service cores, to give a column-free interior. The inherent flexibility of this design was proved when an airline merger took place during construction, necessitating the addition of a further interior court unit and the re-location of several departments. Analysis at the design stage determined that the optimum arrangement of administrative functions was best handled in a two-storey solution, with executive offices and staff on the upper floor and support facilities below. S.O.M. are the all-American architects par excellence. Uncompromising analysis and meticulous execution characterize all their work. Their huge organization not only succeeds in preserving exceptionally high standards of design; it also consistently projects a convincing group personality. Nowhere could one find an expression of the efficiency and wealth of commerce in the twentieth century more apt than in the buildings of S.O.M.; but they also reflect the other side of the coin: the ruthlessness and power of big business and the anonymity of the individual.

Photos: Bill Hedrich, Hedrich Blessing

CONTINENTAL CENTRE, CHICAGO

Architects

C. F. Murphy Associates

This building's direct lineage from the original Chicago school is probably more evident than that of any other building of this type erected recently in the city. Its debt to Mies van der Rohe is equally evident, and it is no coincidence that the two architects most intimately involved in the design are both former students of Mies.

The building's chief virtue (which by some may be considered its chief drawback) lies in its reticence, its willingness to take its place in the urban fabric with unassuming dignity.

It pioneered the use of large spans, which has since become a rapidly evolving trend in American office building design. Whether this trend is always appropriate is open to question, but in this case the generous square bays seem logically conceived to give maximum unobstructed space without undue structural gymnastics.

Photos: Richard Nickel

TOLLESTON GYMNASIUM

Architect

Leonard Klarich

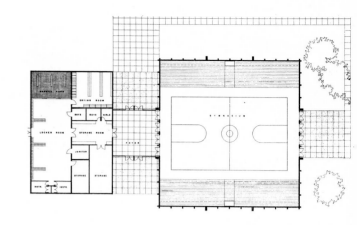

ST LOUIS PLANETARIUM

Architects

Hellmuth, Obata and Kassabaum

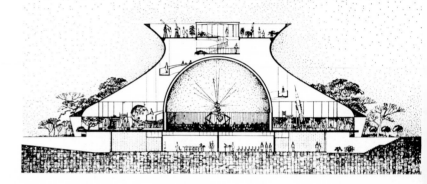

CHEMICAL RESEARCH CENTRE

Architect

Gerald McCue

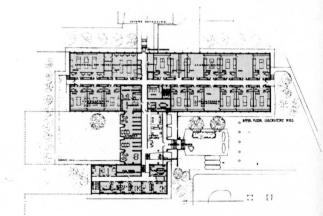

FOOTHILL COLLEGE

Architects

Kump, Masten and Hurd

Photo: Robert Fine

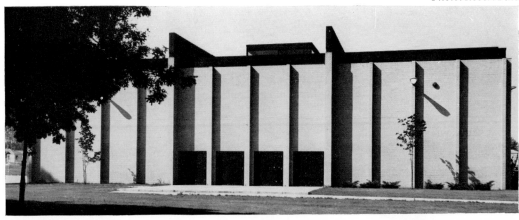

Elegance, formality and simplicity of plan and structure distinguish this gymnasium in Gary, Indiana. The plan developed naturally into a windowless one-hundred-foot square, and a structural system was devised to express logically this requirement. Symmetrical steel cross beams support the major roof loads on heavy brick piers. The minor loads are carried on twenty-five-foot high brick walls which completely enclose the building and are stiffened by projecting ribs.

The brief was to design a building that would be different from any other planetarium in the world. A circular exhibition space surrounds the spherical auditorium for the planetarium projector, and from it a spiral ramp winds up through the height of the interior to an open air space platform on the roof, from which viewers can see the stars through telescopes. The whole complex is enclosed in a single cooling-tower-section, hyperbolic paraboloid.

Photo: Jerry Bragstad

The Stauffer Chemical Building, Richmond, California, forms a nucleus for a larger centre. Research requirements in the chemical industry are fairly stable compared to space development or electronics, and the architects have provided a flexible and workable building. The common areas, such as the library, convey an impression of ease and space in contrast to the practical efficiency of the laboratories. The exterior expresses the concrete frame with formal simplicity.

The faculty buildings, and those for administration and physical education, are grouped in an informal layout of one- and two-storey pavilions throughout the campus. Massive tapered concrete columns are widely spaced and support heavy pitched timber roofs, whose widely overhanging eaves on boldly-expressed chunky rafters protect the footpaths below. The pavilion layout creates a sequence of small-scale courts and patios around larger open spaces.

Photo: Morley Baer

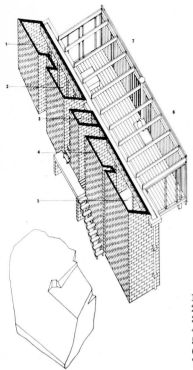

MARVIN HOUSE, CALIFORNIA

Architect

Edward Cullinan

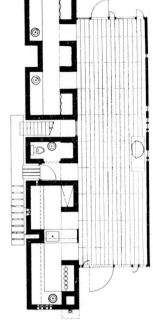

KEY
1 Dressing Room
2 Dressing Room
3 W.C. and Shower
4 Study
5 Kitchen
6 Living
7 Sleeping

Top-lit dressing room
adjacent to sleeping area

Top-lit kitchen
adjacent to dining area

Photos: Jerry Bragstad

The strong sculptural quality of
this house, its harmony with the
site and the compartmenting of the
plan into service and served areas
are its striking characteristics. It
stands on an exposed hillside
overlooking the Pacific and
presents a fortress-like exterior,
austere and private,
echoing the rugged lines of the rock
beside it. The main space is a
single large room, like the gallery
of a Tudor house, in which all the
living, eating and sleeping
activities are concentrated
opposite to the relevant parts of
the service core: the kitchen,
study, bathroom and dressing
rooms. The contrast between
service and served areas is
emphasized not only by a
transition from exposed timber
construction in the living area to
concrete block walls in the service
core, but by a striking contrast in
spatial quality. The generous
proportions of the living areas are
matched by very tight utilitarian
spaces, top-lit, which are rather
too small to accommodate
comfortably the functions they
were designed for. The only views
from the house are through the
two large glazed ends of the living
room and through peep-holes in
concrete blocks laid on edge where
one can glimpse the sea from the
kitchen or a visitor from the study.

BACARDI OFFICES, MEXICO CITY

Architect

Mies van der Rohe

We reject all aesthetic speculation, all doctrine, all formalism. Architecture is the will of an epoch translated into space; living, changing, new. Not yesterday, not tomorrow, only today can be given form. Only this kind of building will be creative.
Create form out of the nature of our tasks with the methods of our time. *This is our task.*
We refuse to recognize problems of form, but only problems of building.
Form is not the aim of our work, but only the result.
Form, by itself, does not exist.
Form as an aim is formalism; and that we reject.
Essentially our task is to free the practice of building from the control of aesthetic speculators and restore it to what it should exclusively be: building.

Mies van der Rohe 1923

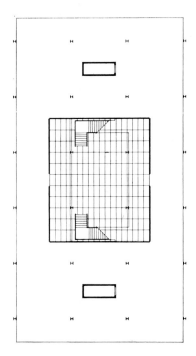

GROUND FLOOR PLAN   FIRST FLOOR PLAN

Photos: Baltazar Korab

No other architect has remained so uncompromisingly faithful to the early tenets of his architectural philosophy as Mies van der Rohe. None more clearly reveals his imitators' failure to re-create his personal and unique magic. Mies's world-wide influence has been a constant source of inspiration; it has also led through disastrous misunderstanding to much of the dead, anonymous architecture that defaces cities all over the world. There is no architecture more depressing than third-rate pseudo-Mies, none more closely attuned to a total architecture of the twentieth century than his own.

As a young man, Mies was in the van of contemporary thought about the implications of technology. He has refined his idea to transcendent perfection. But today the idea itself surely demands refinement—even at the expense of imperfect execution. The primitive technology of standard steel sections, however finely resolved, is surely a crude and outworn instrument, compared to the technological potentialities of today that have yet to contribute to a true architecture, a true art-science of the twentieth century.

BACARDI OFFICES: Interiors

The stark poetry of space reduced to its absolute essentials, simply expressed with superb materials: glass, steel, marble, travertine and mahogany

Photos: Baltazar Korab

MEXICO

Contributing Editor

Eduardo Terrazas

MISSIONARY CHURCH

Architect

Enrique de la Mora

Engineer

Felix Candela

This is one of several churches produced in collaboration by the architect Enrique de la Mora and the engineer Felix Candela. The plan expresses the liturgical movement towards a central altar. The architect has organized the liturgical functions within a rhomboid plan, creating a major and minor space beneath the sweeping canopy of the curved concrete roof. In the major vertex, the choir, missioners and presbytery perform the ceremony; the minor vertex is occupied by the congregation.

The plan, section, structure and liturgical needs are all integrated to achieve a dramatic climax at the top-most point of the vault behind the altar.

The unique structural form was determined by the nature of the sub-soil; a shelf of lava in the middle of the site supports the vault on its short axis, the long axis flying out in a dramatic cantilever. The structure is balanced by a concrete cross that creates a focal point for the main entrance.

The architect collaborated closely with the structural engineer and the artists responsible for the stained glass and low-relief sculptured walls, integrating and directing their work to achieve a unified and consistent statement. Even so, it is hard to reconcile the freedom, lightness and movement of Candela's breathtaking vault with the massive, earth-bound masonry of the enclosing walls.

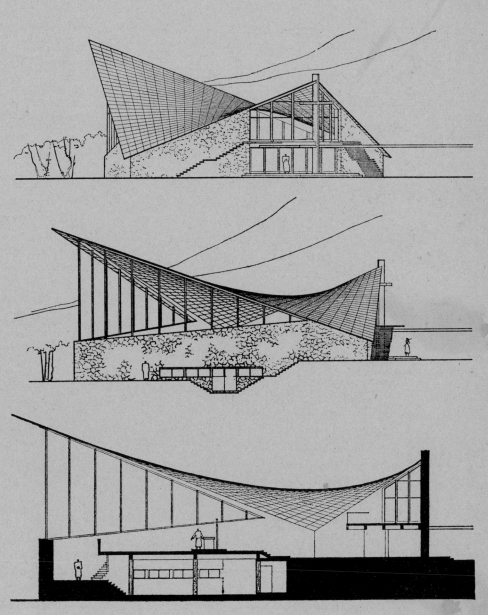

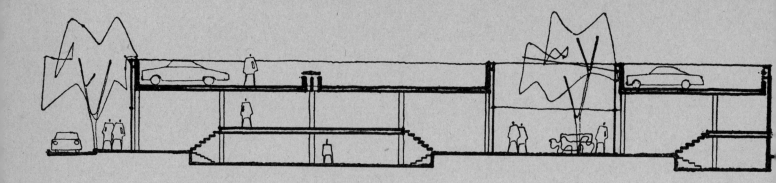

SHOPPING PRECINCT, MEXICO CITY

Architects

Velazquez and Torres

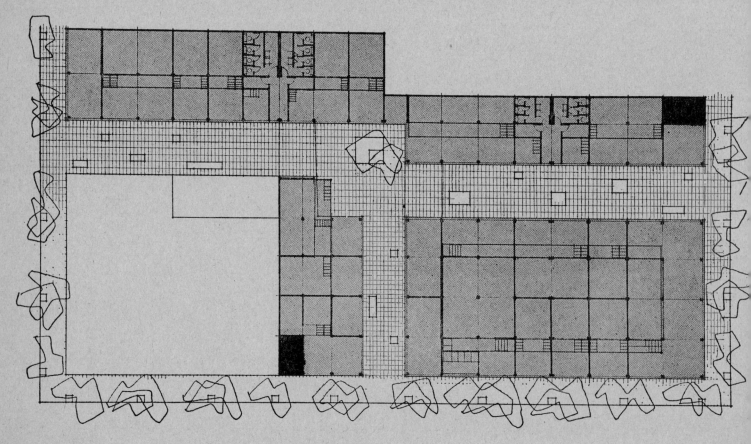

This project is a very successful integration of a shopping centre within an urban area. Three small lots of mean proportions were combined to create a new shopping centre with only pedestrian access. Cars are parked on the roof and cannot be seen from below. An interior plaza and café form a focal space at the centre.

The façades have almost disappeared as dividing elements; inside and outside they dissolve into transparencies and reflections that give their environment a sensation of total space without beginning or end. Big sliding panels of glass open the shops on to the pedestrian street. By creating three levels in each shop the architect has formed a flexible arrangement for displaying different types of merchandise. Tenant's advertising and shop signs are all located behind the glass frontage to maintain the unity of the exterior. Each display brings variety and colour to the severe simplicity of the rectangular framework; points of interest and vitality in the pedestrian corridor of mirrors.

Photos: Héctor Mejía

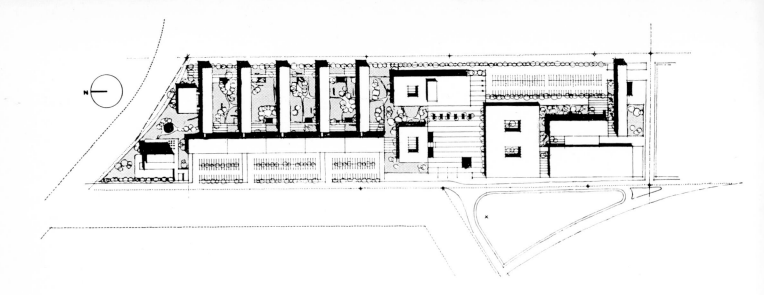

UNIVERSITY, MEXICO CITY

Architects

Alvarez and Carral

New university places and teaching equipment are a primary need for further education in Mexico. In response to this need a group of private organizations have contributed to create this new university. It is located near the University City of Mexico because many of the professors will teach in both places. The new buildings will be constructed in a series of stages of which this is the first, just recently finished. Each stage is a self-contained functional unit. In designing the university for continuous development the architects have provided for the evolution of administrative and educational needs, by creating a system of free spaces uncluttered by structure that can be freely adapted to changing requirements. The aim of the plan is to relate the various departments so that each student will be aware of a variety of disciplines — not confined within the narrow boundaries of his own specialization. The sloped lecture rooms in the largest building provide a focus where professors and students can meet and exchange ideas; the form was designed to encourage contacts of this kind. The east-west buildings contain the specialized studies, but are all linked with the main lecture building.

The free space of the plan is achieved through the use of a limited structural vocabulary: columns, beams, slabs and membranes that can be combined in a variety of ways so that the façades can respond to the needs of solar orientation and to the functional needs of each department without obstructing the internal arrangements.

Photo: Manuel Paz

Photos: Manuel Paz

VENEZUELA

Contributing Editors

Magali Ruz Brewer and Oscar Tenreiro

José María Vargas Medical School, Caracas

Architect

Nelson Douaihi

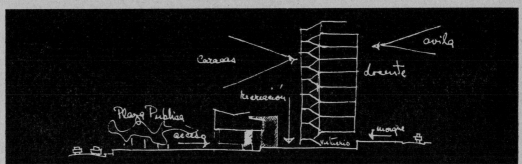

The dignified proportions of this building contrast happily with its environment, a pleasant part of old Caracas where the old houses remain intact. Its simplicity and clarity combine with a reticence that is to be welcomed when so many of our architects are striving for dramatic effect, and in this respect it reflects the return by young Venezuelan architects to a simpler, more direct means of expression.

The materials have been chosen with care. The colouring is discreet and quiet in contrast to the roofs of clay tiles that surround the building. Concrete is the predominant and precisely appropriate material; it is disappointing to see it sadly disguised beneath a thin coating of cement-render that inevitably weakens the appearance of the building. The communal areas on the ground floor below the tower of lecture rooms are based on a system of interlocking hexagons, and have been successfully integrated into the existing square that was remodelled during the construction. These rooms, though spatially interesting, suffer from a lack of scale, and the fragility of the materials used raises doubts about their ability to maintain their appearance over a long period. We feel this is an aspect the architect has failed to resolve. A building for students in Latin America must be more robust if it is to withstand intensive use and receive scanty maintenance.

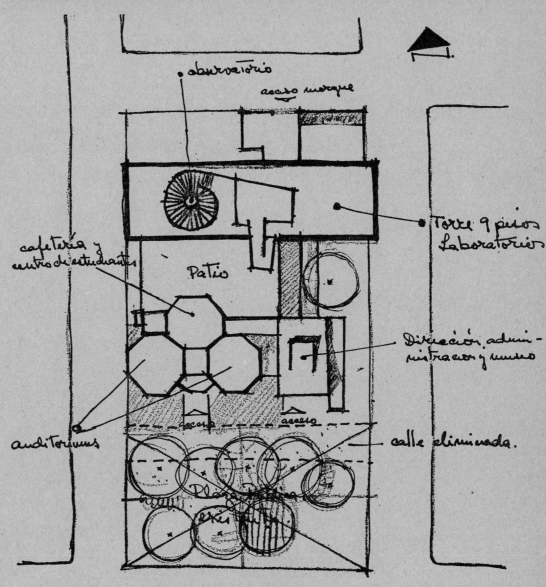

FAMILY HOUSE, CARACAS

Architect

Américo Faillace

The three houses that follow provide a glimpse of the expressive tendencies inherent in the work of young Venezuelan architects. Even in the absence of other examples which might further identify the character of new directions, they reflect the current diversity of new architectural attitudes.

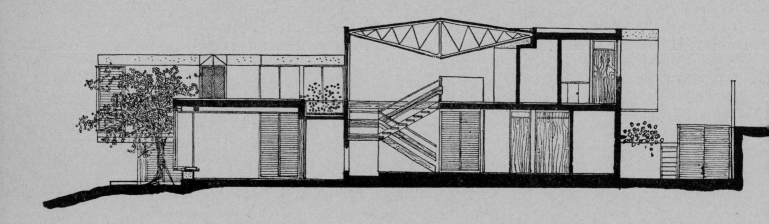

Faillace is an architect closely linked with the popular architecture of Venezuela, which has been called 'folklorist'. He tackles problems with decision and utilizes every available means to create a succession of interior spaces of great interest. This house frames a magnificent view of El Avila hill, and the way in which the plan and section have been integrated with the landscape is most skilful. Materials are used frugally, and the exclusive use of white accentuate texture and the play of light on surfaces. An attempt to break away from a certain conventionalism which he has felt to be present in his previous work has led him to create some bizarre spaces, self-consciously over-designed, and like Hernández, a profusion of superfluous details.

FAMILY HOUSE, CARACAS
Interiors

ARCHITECT'S OWN HOUSE

Architect

JAIME HOYOS

Hoyos is not an architect who looks expressly for innovation. His work reveals tranquillity and maturity, with evident roots in Le Corbusier. He is the most experienced of these three architects, and has successfully developed his highly personal expression from the tentative attempts of his earlier work. This house, built on a steeply sloping site on the fringe of El Avila hill, shows great sobriety — almost austerity — in the use of materials, and in the organization of interior spaces which create a feeling of intimacy and enclosure which heightens the drama of glimpses out across the valley of Caracas.

FAMILY HOUSE, SANTA MONICA, CARACAS

Architect

Henrique Hernández

This house designed by Hernández is an important example of his intention to transcend the rigorous schematics that have dominated the architecture of Venezuela (particularly in the case of houses) and threaten to become a permanent and fixed set of rules. His elaboration of proportions, use and treatment of materials, and sensitive control of spaces all combine with the seriousness of his purpose to give his work an outstanding place in the development of young architects' work in Venezuela. Certain affectations in the search for the interplay of volumes, combined with precocious detailing, reveal a lack of equilibrium arising from his desire to create an impact in reaction to the 'modern-traditional' architecture so common in Venezuela. These tendencies place the seal of the baroque on his buildings but do not obscure the underlying sincerity of their purpose.

SPAIN

Contributing Editor

David Mackay

Two developments of outstanding interest occurred in Spain during 1962. One concerned a crisis in aesthetics and the other a growing awareness of the social responsibility of the profession. The aesthetic crisis coincided with a general reformation in architecture throughout the world, and the fact that it has touched Spain is welcome in that it demonstrates both the validity of the crisis and that Spain can at least match the world intellectually if not technically. The awakening of social responsibility is naturally a slow-moving affair, which should not detract from the essential point that the problem is not only being discovered but that solutions are in the first stage of growth. By concentrating on these two developments, it is hoped to illustrate the healthy and vital position of architecture in Spain today. Actual results are for the future; 1964 should see the completion of many really first-class buildings which may put Spain among the leading countries in quality architecture. The two buildings selected for illustration reveal the end of an epoch, an epoch of a revived rationalism so dear to Spain in the thirties under GATEPAC. The memories of Sert, Torres, Illescas etc. were revived in 1952 by the architects of Group R: Moragas, Gili, Bassó, Bohigas, Martorell, Ribas-Piera, Coderch, Valls and Sostres. After the moral collapse brought about by the disaster of the Civil War, this ginger group rekindled the fire of modern architecture, mounting exhibitions, organizing conferences and above all creating an atmosphere of frank self-criticism by visiting works designed by members of the group. During the ten year life of Group R such buildings as the architect's own house by Moragas, BEA offices by Gili and Bassó, houses in Sitges by Coderch, Valls and Sostres, and the house Guardiola by Martorell and Bohigas, were produced. The greater effort, however, was reserved for the building group, Escorial, designed in 1955 — a rational design showing the first signs of restlessness at the failings of the rationalist creed, by accepting the urban environment instead of rebelling against it. In Madrid, too, the modern movement was revived with some fine buildings.

The other building illustrated is a house designed by the architect Antoni Bonet. This has been selected because in its own personal way it excellently sums up the extent of the cultural intercourse between Spain and South America. The sweeping rationalizations so common to America are to be found in the structural conception, but here tempered with a softening of the lines, achieved by exploiting the vault on its home ground. Owing to the fact that Antoni Bonet is now designing Spain's first new towns at *Mar Menor* (*Murcia*) and *Andalucía la Nueva* (*Málaga*), this building gives a forewarning of what to expect.

ESCORIAL HOUSING DEVELOPMENT, BARCELONA View over Gracia showing the tall block and Gaudí's Sagrada Familia on the skyline

CATALAN COLLEGE OF ARCHITECTS

Architect

Xavier Busquets

First floor ceramic frieze by Picasso

On April 29th, 1962 the new building in the Plaça Nova, opposite the Cathedral in Barcelona and housing the Catalan College of Architects, was inaugurated. Besides being an extraordinary demonstration of competent professional organization, it sparked off an almost violently strong polemic on the aesthetics and functions of architecture and decoration. The building itself, designed by the architect Xavier Busquets, represents a significant victory for modern architecture in Barcelona.

The new building of the College of Architects is the first building to breach the archaism of the gothic quarter. Not surprisingly, it is the object of bitter controversy. Adding fuel to the fire, Xavier Busquets bravely invited the collaboration of Picasso, who spent his boyhood in Barcelona, to design a gigantic frieze around the base of the building. However, controversy did not end there. If in public the discussion has centred around 'functional' or 'traditional' architecture, between intellectuals the controversy has burned fiercely between the designs for the various floors of the interior, each of which was designed by a different architect. It was not that they expressed various personal interpretations of the Modern Movement, as was generally expected, but that for the first time in the close proximity of the same building the current fundamental division of the Modern Movement was brought into sharp relief; on one side 'Idealism' and on the other the 'New-realism'. As this has taken place in their own building, every architect has been forced to enter the controversy by deciding in favour of one side or the other, or to withdraw from it altogether. The two extremes are generally agreed to be: the floor accommodating the dean of the college and his executive suite, designed with the glacial purity of modulism in steel and glass by the 'idealist' architects Tous and Fargas; and the floor accommodating the section dealing with the registration of plans by the so-called 'New-realist' architects Martorell, Bohigas and Mackay:

The 'idealists' are attacked for not being able to move out of the experimental age of the twenties and thirties; of being guilty of formalism in forcing the programme and materials to conform to a rigid arbitrary module; and of attempting finishes demanded by the use of certain materials that are impossible to achieve in an under-industrialized building industry; furthermore, of failing to design in accordance with the country's climatic and economic conditions. The 'New-realists' are attacked for being reactionary, and for being guilty of personalism and historicism bordering on neo-liberty — thus weakening the advance of technology and failing to prepare the country for full industrialization.

The controversy arising from these fundamentally opposed attitudes raged so furiously that an inquiry was published in *Serra D'Or*, in which critics and painters, a sculptor and an architect all expressed their views. It is significant that a piece of modern architecture should promote such lively critical comment amongst the intellectuals of Barcelona.

David Mackay

INTERIORS
1st floor: Vestibule. *Arch:* Xavier Busquets
2nd floor: Library. *Archs:* Giráldez, Lopez and Subias
3rd floor: Information and publications. *Archs:* Monguió and Vayreda
4th floor: Registration and administration. *Archs:* Martorell, Bohigas and Mackay
5th floor: Administration. *Arch:* Moragas
6th floor: Board and committee rooms. *Archs:* Fargas and Tous
7th floor: Club. *Archs:* Correa and Milá
8th floor: Bar and restaurant. *Archs:* Correa and Milá

8th

7th

6th

Photos: F. Catalá Roca

5th

4th

3rd

2nd

1st

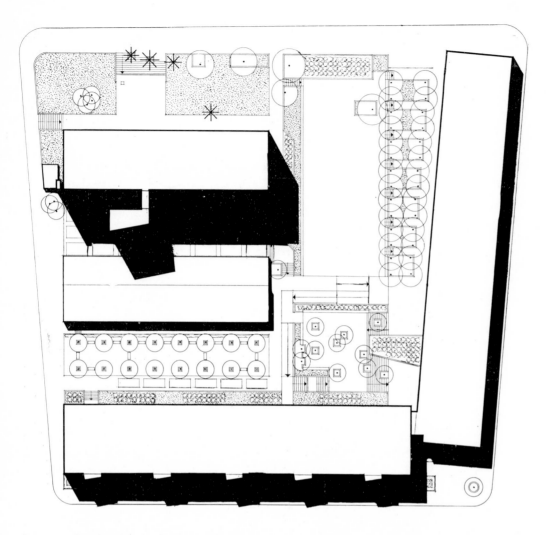

As a result of a competition in 1953, the architects Perpiña and Mitjans, Ribas Casas, Bohigas and Martorell, and Alemany, began in 1955 to design the housing group in *carrer Escorial,* Barcelona. During the succeeding years the project was developed, and in the process achieved fundamental changes in the local planning laws. In urban planning the group is historic in that it has revitalized the decayed Cerdá plan for the Barcelona block by returning to the nineteenth-century planner's original idea of interior gardens. More important still the architects have avoided the space-killing parallel block; instead, the two lower blocks form an open angle to the sun and gardens, and are at the same time parallel to the corresponding streets. To conserve the density allowed by the planning authorities, the rest of the accommodation has been housed in a tall block so situated that it neither dominates the street nor overshadows the two lower buildings — open planning integrated into the urban environment.

Advantage has been taken of the sloping site to break up the gardens into a series of interconnected spaces each with its own character and function always in close relation to the architecture. It is difficult to find fault with this outstanding work and perhaps the only really questionable item is the situation of the commercial block within the shadow of the tall block. The flats over the shops get no sun at all, and this within a site dedicated to open planning. On the other hand, this small block does greatly assist in creating agreeable spaces about the buildings. A criticism can also be held against the clients for not going far enough in the social work of the group; surely at least a nursery school should have been provided. However, it must be remembered that building societies are notoriously conservative and this one should at any rate be congratulated on undertaking a bold experiment.

HOUSING GROUP, CARRER ESCORIAL, BARCELONA

Architects

Perpiña, Mitjans, Casas, Bohigas, Martorell and Alemany

Photo: T.A.F.

Open planning in the urban townscape

Covered play area protected from the sun through which
the busy street outside penetrates into the garden oasis

Photo: F. Catalá Roca

CARRER ESCORIAL The variety of character and treatment of different blocks

Photos: F. Catalá Roca

Composite view from the sea

LA RICARDA, A HOUSE BY THE SEA

Architect

Antoni Bonet

Photo: F. Catalá Roca

Photo: Katzenstein

La Ricarda *has brought the scale of South America to Europe and reintegrated it with the tradition of the mother country. The architectural result is extraordinarily satisfying. Antoni Bonet is one of the few architects who could have brought it off. Born in 1913 and educated in Barcelona, he moved to Argentina as a result of the Spanish Civil War.* La Ricarda *was actually designed from the other side of the Atlantic. Basically the house consists of a vault 30 ft × 30 ft repeated twelve times. The vault has been kept low, in scale with the small Mediterranean pine, and the enclosing walls are either transparent or semi-transparent, allowing a free interchange between the interior and exterior spaces. Thus elements proper to the house extend out to become porches, and the garden has either been drawn in towards the house or actually introduced into it.*

Photo: F. Catalá Roca

BRAZIL

Contributing Editor

David Crease

Photos: Monica Lehmann

BRASILIA

Master Plan: Lucio Costa

Architect: Oscar Niemeyer

Structure of the unfinished Cathedral, Brasilia

Brasilia has now reached the stage where one stops thinking about it as an architectural monument and begins to ask whether, as a place for people to live in, it is really beginning to acquire the internal vitality of a real city. It is still not an easy place to live in, but it does have a considerable amount of city life. Already two hundred thousand people are living in the Federal District, with perhaps fifty to one hundred thousand within a loose area around the master plan. These people, who have been uprooted from their lives elsewhere, have to establish new social links and friendships and, although the adjustment is bound to take time, they already regard themselves as citizens of Brasilia.

The fact that Brasilia has been very formally planned and monumentally conceived to give it the character of a national capital has created certain disadvantages. It was deliberately started from the centre in order to grow outwards, and the outward development has gone on in a rather scattered way. Even though the bus services are quite good you have to travel quite a long way to your work, and on the way you go through large chunks that just have not been built yet. The corollary to this situation is that in the neighbourhoods themselves family life is perfectly liveable without transport. The idea of the *super-quadras* is based on classical neighbourhood planning principles; everything you need for the daily life of the family is within walking distance and you need not cross any major traffic route. Of course such a self-contained life in a *super-quadra* is not enough. The downtown area, the cosmopolitan atmosphere of bright lights, night clubs and restaurants has only just started to be built, but I defy anyone to build a city of any sort that Brazilians cannot turn into a very lively place indeed.

It is very difficult in a city for half a million people not to lose the visual identity of the plan, because of sheer size. Already you can see Brasilia as a whole. It is a very great experience to come driving up from Bella Horizonte or São Paulo for about twelve hours through almost uninhabited country; suddenly, you come over the rim of the hills and see this wonderful city standing there like a mirage.

Brasilia has built up a human base on which it can progress. The original conception of mixed classes and income levels within each *super-quadra* has not really been put into practice, although the idea has not been abandoned. The monumental government buildings in the centre had top priority, and it was essential to build up a labour force for the construction. On the other hand, there was no capital for a low cost housing programme for the labourers. People came swarming in, and were either accommodated in construction companies' wooden camps or they had to fend for themselves. Brasilia was faced right from the start with the problem of shacks and shanty towns that are a part of the life of Latin America. The shanty town community grew

Panorama of Ministries, Congress building and Cathedral in the heart of Brasilia

Photos: Monica Lehman

The Palace of the President and small chapel

up and took root so firmly that it has now been officially declared a satellite town! In fact three or four more satellites have since been created in the Federal District.

Brasilia is first and foremost the administrative capital but it is also the centre of a growing region and an intellectual centre as well. For the population to be balanced and reasonably self-contained, an area has also been laid out for services and light industry. Heavy industry is positively discouraged.

One object behind the whole concept of Brasilia was to create a centre of government independent of the pressures and tensions of the established towns, but it was also intended to help open up the relatively undeveloped Brazilian hinterland. In addition to the city itself, a road has been built right through the jungle from Brasilia to the mouth of the Amazon, and another links the capital with the far west. These roads are fulfilling their function of colonizing the interior. One hundred thousand people have already gone to live up the Brasilia-Bel Air highway. They are granted land on easy terms and move in at once to start cultivating it. Their food production has undoubtedly given a real boost to the development of the region.

Access to President's Palace across a pool to the main entrance

The first buildings put up in Brasilia by Oscar Niemeyer attracted a great deal of interest, but what of the architectural quality of the ordinary buildings now going up? The general level is good without being distinguished. The texture of the town depends much more on the planning than on the architecture, and there is no doubt that many of the new buildings are monotonous and disappointing. Niemeyer's buildings are great works, but there are other architects who have also made a good contribution to the urban scene. Glauco Campelo is possibly the best young architect and José da Souza Reis has designed a very good building for the metereological observatory. There is also a very good team of architects who work for the Bank of Brazil, which has been a great supporter of Brasilia, and build a lot there.

By contrast, the *super-quadras* have been built up in considerable numbers and in many cases are architecturally insensitive and heavy-handed. They were produced in great haste by a very reduced team of architects, and the planners hope that more architects will come in with new ideas for the majority of *super-quadras* that still remain to be built. A good deal more variety is to be hoped for. Each *super-quadra* is surrounded by a belt of trees which will give the whole city a new form of cellular structure. Within each cell considerable elasticity is permitted.

Brasilia is no longer a symbol; it is a reality, and it has already played a very definite part in Brazilian politics. When President Quadros resigned there was a very difficult political situation in Brazil, with the threat of civil war. During the crisis the Congress was able to function coolly and arrived at a solution acceptable to everybody, something that might not have been possible surrounded by an atmosphere of mob violence in Rio. At such times of crisis, Brasilia really takes its place as the capital of a nation. Now it will grow. How it grows is an architectural and social matter; as a political issue it is dead. It would be difficult to point to any other experiment being conducted on such a scale to deal with the problems of our new urban environment.

From an interview between David Crease and J. M. Richards

Double-height interior of Planalto Palace

Twin-slab Congress building seen through the structure of the Planalto Palace

Photos: Monica Lehmann

Dome-shaped Hall for the Upper House and
saucer-shaped Hall for the Lower House, with Ministries beyond

Mezzanine of three-level bus station linked by escalators

Congress building from the
Plaza of the Three Powers

Twin-slab Secretariat built
over the lake

PORTUGAL

Contributing Editor

Luiz Sarmento de Carvalho e Cunha

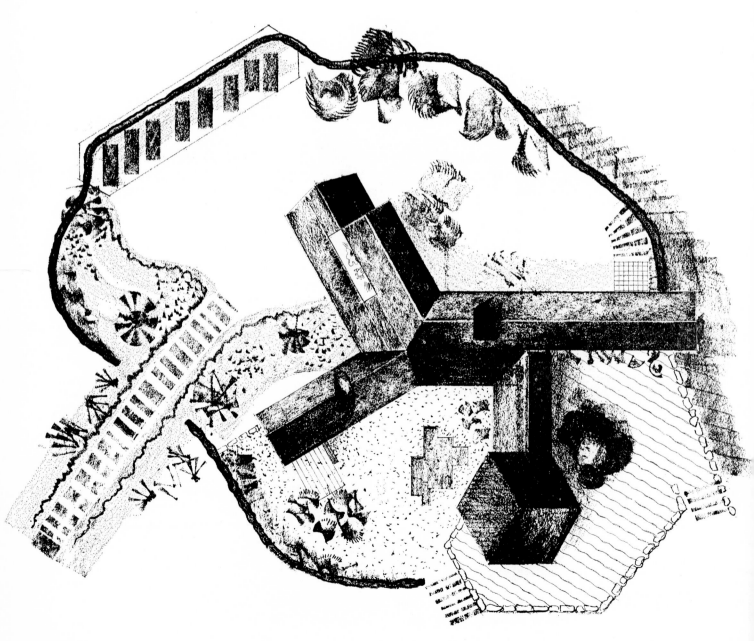

The Search for an Authentic Architecture

For the first volume of *World Architecture* I have decided to concentrate on the north of Portugal, particularly the Oporto region, hoping to complete the picture with work from the centre and the south of the country in the second issue. Restricting this first panorama to the north will still enable me to present a picture of the evolution of Portuguese architecture. Ideas which germinated in the north later spread to the rest of the country. In order to understand the present situation it is important to point out that the most influential architects in the period between 1945–1955 adopted a line of action based on the principles of C.I.A.M. Viana de Lima and Fernando de Távora took part in the congresses and spread their ideas among the younger generation still at school. Viana de Lima also put up some of the best buildings at this time. Their most important characteristic was a rigorous functional programme acknowledging the international style that was current through the influence of Le Corbusier. Developments in Brazilian architecture also exerted a powerful influence because of the close relationship between our two countries.

At the same time the impact of a European cultural evolution characterised by the work of Scandinavian and Italian architects, and the critical appraisal of Frank Wright's architecture were being felt.

So it is in this climate of influences that we must place the most recent work, because the foreign influences are weakening to give place not to a Portuguese modern architecture but to a better adaptation to the particular, human and geographical conditions of Portugal; and this is the aspiration of those who conscientiously work today: to create authentic architecture rather than a national style. In this context the early work of Fernando de Távora, dating from 1955, gives reality to certain ideas which on the one hand were the result of his experience in C.I.A.M., and on the other hand expressed new thinking of his own. The characteristics of his architecture at this time have remained in his more recent work, and have influenced those younger architects who were working towards the same ideals.

At the same time Januario Godinho's development was very personal, although he aimed at similar objectives. His construction of a series of *pousadas*, and all the other buildings for a hydro-electric scheme reveal careful study based on a very complete knowledge of the conditions. All the buildings are designed to grow in a harmonious relationship to the landscape. Godinho's work is of special interest because he belongs to the generation which introduced modern architecture to Portugal. He does not belong to any particular group or school of thought and so goes in a direction independent from the majority, yet his solutions correspond in many ways to the ideas of the younger architects.

SADA OF PISÕES SITE PLAN
t: Januário Godinho
'pousada' is like a small private
l for the personnel of a hydro-
tric scheme.

The most interesting architecture in recent years, although fulfilling structural functional requirements, clearly reveals other intentions. One notices a special interest in the integration of the buildings with the environment. It is not only a question of harmony with the landscape, but also, and especially, of relating architecture to the historical, social and cultural environment.

The new interest in social aspects is reflected in architecture, and in 'habitat' in particular and has led to a re-examination of Portugal's historical past. This re-examination has created respect for tradition, attention to local characteristics and sympathy towards the proportions, materials and colours that have characterized Portuguese architecture in the past.

There is also a renewed interest in popular architecture. Godinho, for instance, enjoys telling us how at the beginning of his career he went through the whole country observing buildings and urban groups, and photographing them to capture the real essence of Portuguese architecture.

With the rediscovery of Portuguese architecture the new generation became conscious of the artificiality of those architects who used structural techniques and technical processes which were too far advanced for the capabilities and organization of the traditional building industry, and preferred instead to rationalize traditional techniques. Even so, the scale of our construction programme will soon demand that the potentialities of pre-fabrication and industrialization receive serious thought.

Schools: Fernando de Távora and Viana de Lima

The primary school of Fernando de Távora in Villa Nova de Gaia is based on traditional methods of construction in which austere structural systems, although handled in a refined and sensitive way, still reflect their origin in popular Portuguese architecture. Unconcealed timber roofs show patient attention to structural details. The flow of space in the interior, staircases leading to changes of level and subtle illumination create a variety of spatial experience which contrasts vividly with the spaces usually found in our schools. Its relation to the landscape is perfect, particularly considering the difficulty of integrating it into a residential quarter of negligible architectural interest.

Boa Nova

The restaurant at Boa Nova near Oporto, by Siza Vieira, stands on an exposed site, surrounded by rocks not far from the sea, with a beautiful little chapel nearby. Siza's construction amidst the rocks creates a drama between the building and nature, which is unusual and wonderful. The building and the landscape belong together; even the chapel which is small and modest and might have been spoilt, gains something from the association. The restaurant is entered through narrow paths between the rocks that remind us of all the enchanting mysteries of unexplored paths, and open up into the large rooms overlooking the sea. This glorious landscape, so full of life and motion is brilliantly unified with the internal space.

As we discover all the subtle relationships of ceiling heights, changes of level and perfection of detail, we are constantly reminded of the uniqueness of the site and of Siza Vieira's extraordinary capacity to create original forms.

The quality of the materials he uses, marble, pavings, the comfortable warmth of the timber, the nostalgic green copper roofs, combine in perfect harmony and create effects of surprise and delight while the forms of great plastic beauty have an overall unity which remains consistent throughout the design.

Luiz Cunha

Photos: Luiz Cunha

PRIMARY SCHOOL, BRAGANÇA

Architect

Viana de Lima

*The Portuguese government has
made an effort to provide the
country with improved teaching
facilities and has made a valuable
contribution although the
pedagogic evolution has been
only moderate. This is evident in
the poor quality of many official
projects. The best results have
come from those architects who in
carrying out municipal work have
remained independent. Even so
they are severely restricted by an
obligatory and traditional
arrangement of spaces that is out
of date, and prevents the creation
of new methods of internal
organization to reflect new
methods of teaching.*

*The primary school of Viana de
Lima shows that it is at least
possible to create architecture
within the limiting conditions of
official programmes and budgets.
The composition is planned around
a central space which can be used
as a covered playground, or
adapted to form a multi-purpose
space which the children can use
in a variety of ways. The building
is an interpretation of local
conditions based on unspecialized
techniques and capable of
repetition on different sites.*

*The objective is to replace official
school-types with single buildings
that take the greatest possible
advantage of the small space the
budget permits.*

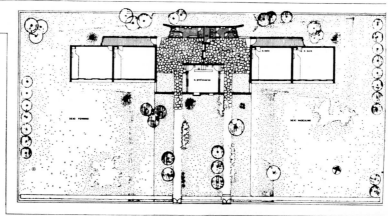

PRIMARY SCHOOL, VILA NOVA DE GAIA

Architect

Fernando de Távora

Photos: J. Gigante

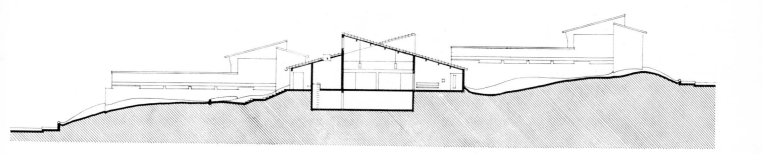

PLAN OF THE GROUND FLOOR
1 Porch
2 Entrance
3 Staff room
4 Class room
5 Covered playground
6 Playground
7 Storage
8 Kitchen
9 Multi-purpose room

Photo: F. Aroso

For a long time I thought architecture to be something different, special, sublime, and belonging to another world, as if it were an unapproachable vestal virgin, aloof, ideal, only known and understood by a chosen few. An architect for me was either a god-like genius or a zero. I could see no link between a small hut and the most famous architectural masterpiece, nor could I see any connection between a brick-layer and an architect. They were different, entirely separate things and people.
This mystical concept of archi-tecture and of the role of the architect caused me much suffering. I felt it would be impossible for me to conceive buildings as pure and untouchable as vestal virgins, because I knew I was no genius.

(continued)

Photos: F. Aroso

Time went by. I saw buildings and I knew other architects. I learned that a building is more than a beautiful drawing, more than a good photograph taken on a sunny day from a well chosen viewpoint: I verified that in the end all architects were men — some good, some better, some worse. And so I gradually realized that architecture is above all an event, which like all events are part of the life of men, and like them are conditioned by many uncertainties — and the awesome vestal virgin became for me instead a symbol of life.

I found architecture to be something which I or any other man can do a little better, a little worse — terribly uncertain, as chained to circumstances as a tree is rooted in the earth. And the myth was shattered, and I saw the hut and the masterpiece as part of a whole, and I understood the connection between the bricklayer and the master architect. Architecture then appeared to me as a great force, a force born out of the earth and out of men, bound by a thousand strings to the varieties of reality, a force capable of contributing vigorously to the felicity of its environment.

Both in its cause and effect it is a weapon at the service of man for the creation of his own happiness. It was with these thoughts in mind that I conceived this school. I tried to consider everything — from the strong winds that blow over the site, to the stones and blocks of the walls; from the enforced official requirements to the well-being of the children and teachers, from the building costs to the fall of the ground. But as well as attempting not to miss any detail, I tried to organize the conditioning factors and integrate them in a whole which would be more than an addition of distinct parts.

Like a tree this building has its roots, it has its moments of beauty, it shelters and shades those who use it, and having been born and been used, it will one day die. It was not for me any longer a matter of an unapproachable vestal virgin but of a small and simple building done by men for men to use.

Fernando de Távora

RESTAURANT BY THE SEA, BOA NOVA

Architect

Siza Vieira

Photos: F. Aroso

*The competition run by the
Matosinhos Municipality for the
new restaurant at Boa Nova
allowed the building to be sited at
the discretion of the competitors.
I knew that part of the rocky coast
well: the slow rising hill on the
land side, the naked ground
marked by large loose rocks on the
sea side. Fernando de Távora had
already conceived the general
layout and made the road study
for the area.
He thought that the sudden
transition between the land and
the sea stressed by a small
platform would be the ideal site for
the building.
I wanted to avoid the constant
imposition of a view — a restaurant
is not a belvedere.
In the entrance, the wooden
ceiling splits and fragments the
view so that the meeting of the
sky and the sea and of the earth*

and the sky are seen separately.
In this building the interior space
is not the negative of the outer
shape. The wooden ceiling is set
free and models the interior
volume without, however, breaking
through the outer form.
There is a tension between the
meeting of outside and inside.
I was not able to master fully the
space of the main lounge. The
furnishing I am now studying
attempts to eliminate or at least
soften this and other defects.
Quite naturally, during this work
I undertook to analyse the
adjoining very old chapel and
study the free and true way in
which it becomes part of the scene.
I became aware that simplicity is
only rarely to be found amongst
the builders of our time. I became
aware of how difficult but how
necessary it is to find it again.
Siza Vieira

MOZAMBIQUE

Contributing Editor

Amancio d'Alpoim Guedes

PYRAMIDAL KINDERGARTEN

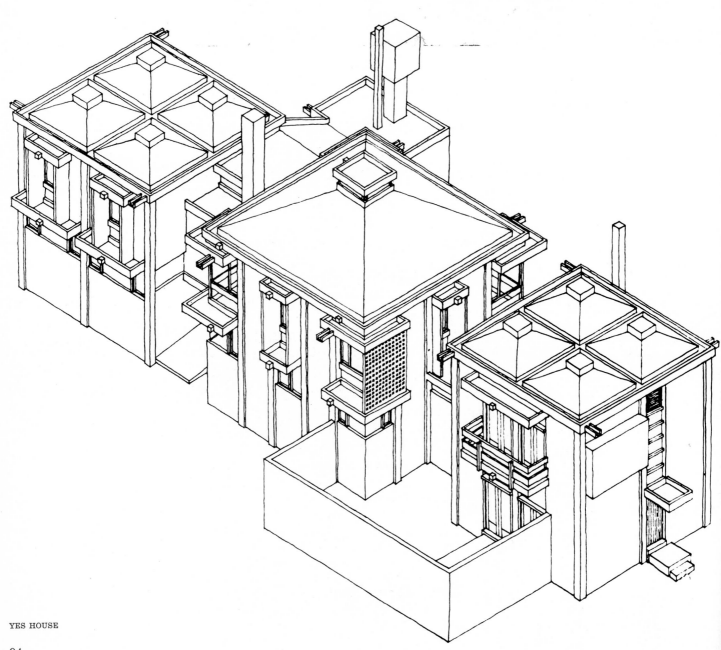

YES HOUSE

The American Egyptian Style

On the progeny of the pyramidal kindergarten and the yes house followed by a short interrogation.

Styles at first used to move slowly and live long, one at a time. Later there were 57 simultaneous varieties, all old. Then some showed others how some could invent their own ways, but the strain was too much for most, and the new died just before it became the style.

Soon after, almost everybody who had been watching the new got together in white, flat-topped uniforms and started the one way.

Anybody who wasn't in, was dead.

On the road, the whitest amongst them invented new rules, merrily approved and readily borrowed — to look the wrong way we all wore blinkers — to be in the wrong place we all pulled ourselves up on thin legs. The legs got steadily fatter and the voices were so many that we were all soon back where others had started.

When the big fog came, some said it was nice and in Italy they dug up the dead but Kahn spoke out through his ducts and he said that buildings would henceforth be what they wanted to be and many rejoiced because buildings were going to be what they needed to become — aesthetic and well served; because buildings were at last going to find their own faces.

Paradoxically buildings everywhere became more and more like Kahn had wanted his own to be — born old and overfed. And so began the American Egyptian style, hot today and gone tomorrow—because architects are all eyes and no ears.

The pyramidal kindergarten and the yes house are both members of the world wide progressive family, both isolated little *machines à émouvoir*, both yes-ing with a foreign accent.

Interrogation

1 How can buildings become what they need to become, some pretty, some dark, others ugly, some fat and clever — real — like people?
2 Where is the idea greater than the sight?
3 When will architects start wanting people in their buildings?

Amancio d'Alpoim Guedes

THE PYRAMIDAL KINDERGARTEN or
SHELTER FOR SMALL ONES

Architect

Amancio d'Alpoim Guedes

Lourenço Marques is the capital city of Mozambique. It is hot and humid for half of the year and the sun shines and glares almost every day. The town grows big, fast. Like most towns it is more and more two towns. One permanent, flowered, serviced, painted and tarred. The other a clutter of huts made out of scrap, tin, mud and reeds; rusty, without water, without night light, without drainage; a labyrinth of narrow and sandy passages. The shelter for small ones of Our Lady of the Conception is a nursery school, run by nuns with some lay help. It cares for the children of the permanent town. Nobody cares for the others.

The shelter stands on the edge of the new, cramped and chic suburb near to the old shooting range. In the suburb, Swiss chalets, folksy houses, Brazilian memories and innumerable other imports confront one another across pocket size gardens and back yards.

The building was meant for 180 small ones; it now looks after 300 children and babies and they are everywhere — in the staff quarters, in the entrance hall, in one of the dormitories and where they should be. The children are taken to and from home in the school's own buses. The buses park in the entrance hall. Rarely are buildings used exactly for what they were meant.

The chapel's sky eye

Only the first stage is built. The second stage consisted originally of a large hall, dining room and kitchen. This I have now re-done to be able to take in more children and still try to be a hall sometimes.

The building consists of a spine of rooms opening onto small play courts. Upstairs are the staff quarters. Underneath the big pyramid is a chapel; the three small pyramids are outdoor toy stores. The end one, on legs, will be the children's entrance when the street is made. The triplet pyramids still to be built will be the hall.

The building is white and bright blue and a little dirty grey. When the trees grow, the site will become a courtyard bounded by a soft big green wall of shade.

I hope later, when the newness rubs off and the children know it well, that the shelter will become many chambers of delights, many pyramids of joy where each day is a feast; and that in the central playground we will still build the pillar of smiles.

Now, as it stands, it is a carcass for indefinite wants, a platform for temporary needs, some spaces for make-shift alternatives. Now the pyramids by the shooting range stand haunted by factory-painted plaster saints, pot-planted and thoroughly venetian-blinded.

Amancio d'Alpoim Guedes

Good morning, Mr Architect

View from south east

Swings and bus entrance

View from south west — morning

Pre-cast concrete block screen

Photos: Amancio d'Alpoim Guedes

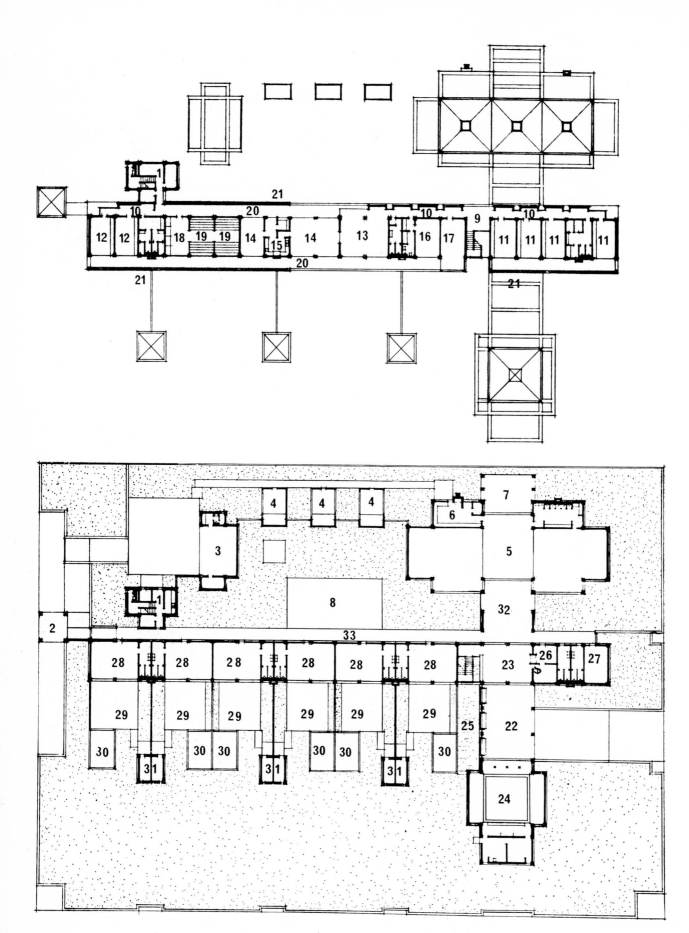

Photos: Amancio d'Alpoim Guedes

KEY

1 Service block and stairs
2 Bus entrance
3 Buses' garage
4 Chicken run (to be built)
5 Hall (to be built)
6 Kitchen (to be built)
7 Pergola (to be built)
8 Terrace and playground
   (to be built)
9 Hall
10 Passage
11 Nuns' dormitory
12 Servants' dormitory
13 Lounge
14 Dining room
15 Kitchen
16 Mother Superior's room
17 Study
18 Laundry
19 Drying room
20 Verandah
21 Concrete block screen
22 Entrance
23 Hall
24 Chapel
25 Pool
26 Administration
27 Doctor
28 Playroom
29 Play terrace and verandah
30 Sand pit
31 Outdoor toy store
32 Porch
33 Access verandah

Bay window of nuns' study

View of chapel pyramid and toy store pyramid from verandah

Sing-song in the entrance hall with potted plants and
St Vincent of Paris in the corner

Children and nuns in the chapel

Detail showing bay window, water tank and two drainage stacks

Chapel and pews

Detail of pews designed by the architect

Junction between column and beam

The chapel's sky eye

Photos: *Amancio d' Alpoim Guedes*

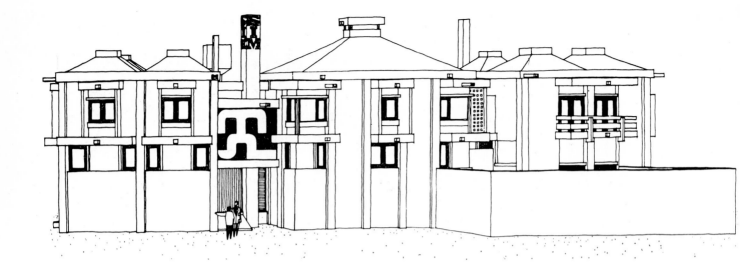

THE YES HOUSE *for Robin Spence who said yes all along*

Architect

Amancio d'Alpoim Guedes

The yes house is an administration building with a caretaker's flat at the side. It is a new head for an old factory. In the factory they make soap, squeeze oil out of nuts and cook greases to make everybody more beautiful. In the office they make money.

The new building says yes on all sides. *Sim* is yes in Portuguese.

First I made a trade mark for them, later we changed the name and made new letterheads and cheques, then I invented the new building. Ferreira da Silva, a small builder, built it. I saw it becoming almost every day. Now we are busy changing the wrappers and the size, shape and smell of what the factory makes. That's what architecture is all about. We must become part of what we do.

The building was conceived as a functional and economic structure — a strong image capable of retaining its entity in the chaotic half-slummy, half-industrial environment.

It is made of patchy reinforced concrete cast in crude old wood shuttering and painted white, with plastered cement block walls. The floors are finished in grey cement grano. The opening casements are in local red hardwood, varnished. The fixed glass is set into plaster and concrete rebates. The concrete pyramidal roofs are finished in grano and white-washed. The building is yellow, grey and white, with the signs and trade mark in black and white.

I wanted to do a stark, humble, ugly, smiling sort of a building, marked with gigantic black signs and pretty letters. I wanted to do a building that would survive being dirty — streaked, stained, altered, soiled by time and the passage of people — a building dented by bullets, with chickens scratching in the back yard.

I wanted it to be a building saying yes to all men.

Amancio d'Alpoim Guedes

Yes!

104

The Yes House in its environment

Photos: Amancio d'Alpoim Guedes

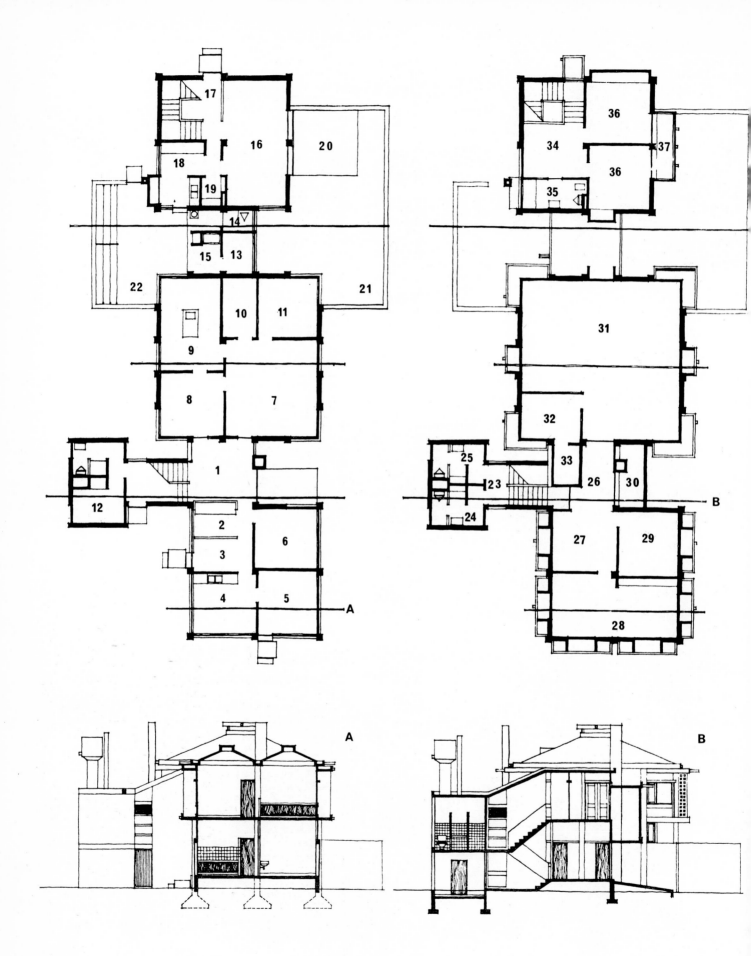

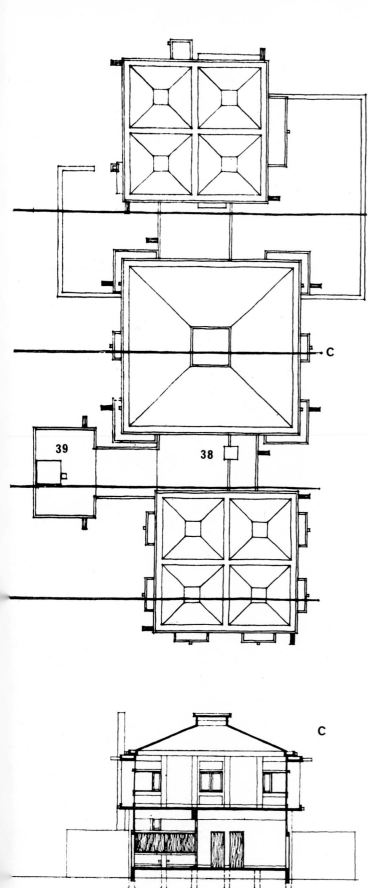

Mealie boys

Photo: Amancio d'Alpoim Guedes

Photos: Amancio d'Alpoim Guedes

Corner detail

Left Detail of corner window

Right Entrance

Back elevation

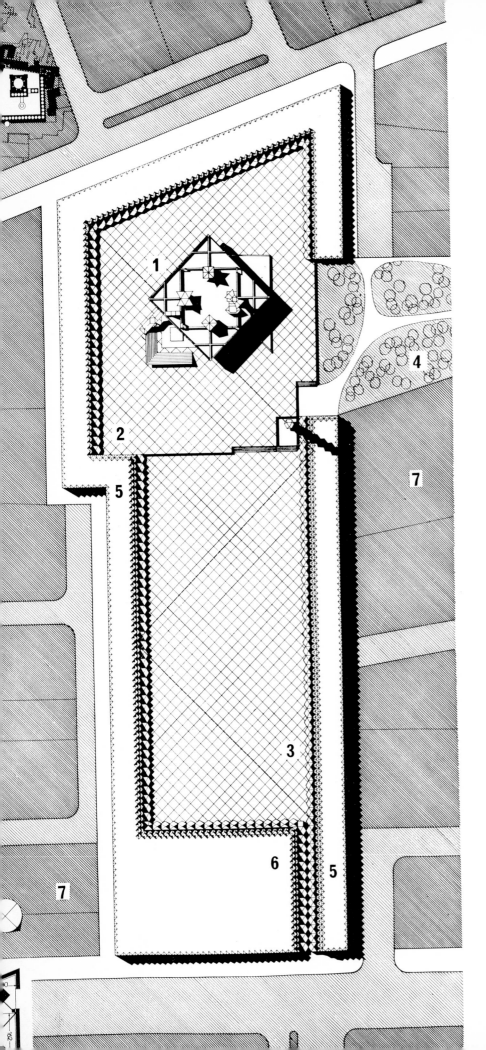

ISRAEL

Contributing Editor

Ram Karmi

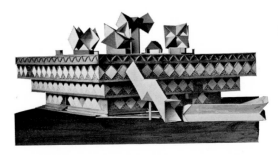

BAT YAM TOWN HALL AND CIVIC CENTRE
Archs: Neumann, Hecker and Sharon

Bat Yam is an industrial town on
the Mediterranean coast, south of
Tel-Aviv, with a present population
of 60,000. The proposed Civic
Centre will be at the future
geographic centre of the town. At
present it is on the southern fringe,
about 300 yards from the sea. It
takes the form of a long rectangle
divided into a lower piazza for
shopping and entertainment, and an
upper piazza for administration,
with the town hall in the centre.
The enclosing buildings consist of
two storeys of flats and offices over
a ground floor of shops and cafés,
whose entrances are shaded by a
continuous pergola built of pre-cast
concrete elements. All entrances to
the central space are kept narrow
to preserve the sense of enclosure.
But to the west side of the town hall
the piazza opens on to a green
boulevard leading to the sea. The
Civic Centre is in the middle of an
area which will be of a fairly high
density, with three-storey housing
punctuated by tower-blocks.
The Town Hall, which is in the
shape of an inverted ziggurat, is
based on a 'cubo–octahedral' space
packing unit. The building is at 45°
to the rectangular piazza and its
structural grid is at 45° to its square
plane. This diagonal grid is repeated
in plan and on elevation, giving
unity to the design. Each of the
three storeys is cantilevered on the
one beneath and protects it from
direct sun and rain. The area
surrounding the building is always
shaded and forms a natural
transition from the exterior piazza
to the interior hall.

Immigration and the Search for Identity

Since the state of Israel was founded fifteen years ago, the population has trebled, and housing is therefore the dominant preoccupation of most architects here; but besides being a sort of speeded-up microcosm of the world population explosion, the pressure is heightened by the fact that the bulk of this increase is due to immigration. People have come from over sixty countries, speaking different languages, having different ways of life and expecting different standards of living; all they share is the need for a home and the desire to identify themselves with Israel.

The State undertook to perform the apparently impossible feat of creating a nation out of this mêlée, an undertaking that involved enormous economic, social, educational and industrial problems. After fifteen years of struggle, it can be said that everybody has somewhere to live, a job, and a fairly high standard of living. In order to achieve this in such a short time, many things have had to be sacrificed; perhaps too many, and it is time now to pause and do the accounting.

As they look around them, the younger architects feel dissatisfied with most of what has been and is now being built, particularly with the town planning. They do not feel that real homes have been created for the people — merely roofs over their heads. The new towns, the social centres, the blocks of flats, all appear meaningless when it comes to actually living in them. The majority of architects and planners seem to have lost contact with the realities of living and failed to provide for the basic needs of the immigrant — a home and a social identity.

Garden cities in the desert, the rational architecture of the four functions, these and many other credos have been transplanted here and all have failed; the drifting sands pile up in the communal open spaces, commuters trek from one zoned function to another, the sun slams down into the vast deserted piazza and only the newly planted trees (about which happily all Israelis have a fixation) give shade and comfort to the eye. These credos have resulted in towns that feel at best like a wild-west stage set and at worst like something out of Kafka. We do not believe in them. However, it is by examining the ways in which they have failed that we can perhaps discover the needs of the people involved. They are places which are not places; there is no feeling of arrival, of entering, being in, and leaving. One is always expecting something to happen, and it never does; just neighbourhood after neighbourhood of organized

KEY TO CIVIC CENTRE

1 Town Hall
2 Upper Piazza
3 Lower Piazza
4 Pedestrian link to the sea
5 Shops and offices
6 Community building
7 Existing zoning for three-storey housing

111

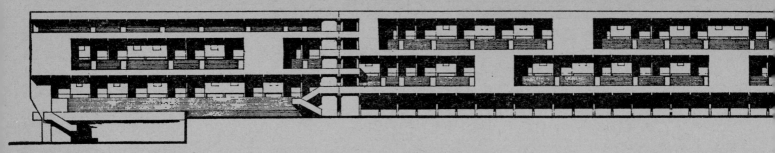

nowhere, with nothing to belong to, no sense of place or of specialness, no spatial possibility for the unpremeditated event, the spontaneous action or fortuitous meeting; nothing in fact but an additive series of pretty surfaces, with flats facing north/south in parallel blocks, where it is easy to find yourself suddenly in somebody else's flat by mistake.

Inside the dwelling itself, great progress has been made with the planning, which is probably, within the limits imposed on price and area by the administration, better than in most countries. That problems of how to relate these dwellings remain so completely unsolved is perhaps because nothing like so much real thinking has been done on this subject; it is the sort of thing that seems of secondary importance initially when one is trying to house a lot of people quickly, and only later does one realize that it is of primary importance to discover exactly the way the dwellings form a community, because this is the actual reason for housing them at all.

In Israel housing has been stacked, staggered and spread in a variety of more or less ingenious geometric arrangements; forming endless sequences of virtually meaningless compositions, their surfaces decorated with graphic designs unrelated to the spaces behind, to progressions of human scale or social identity. To inhabit such an environment is not just to become anonymous, but to cease to exist at all.

Young architects in Israel do not form a coherent or tightly knit group, but what I have tried to show in the buildings illustrated is that we are all trying, each in his own way of thinking and working, to resolve the problems I have described: to give new immigrants a feeling of homecoming, of belonging in their new land, with their own habitat in an environment which stimulates the blending together of their many different social patterns so that the identity and culture of this new nation can grow and take form.

In the work that has begun to fill the void left by the failure of imported theories from the earlier years of the modern movement, certain tendencies can now be distinguished of which the buildings illustrated are in some ways typical. Within the colossal recent building boom, the work of certain young architects, although small in volume and not yet in all ways resolved, has begun to have a wider influence and to show evidence of new directions. Above all, there is a concern with the environment of the fabric of urban living as a whole, and not merely with the design of isolated buildings. (It is perhaps worth remarking that it is surprising how little has been done to produce building systems which use standard elements capable of being put together to give non-standard results; especially surprising with such a constantly pressured housing programme.) Much of this work falls into one of three types: the first group may be seen as an act of faith for Rationalism and International Architecture. It does not try to exploit or distort any element beyond its functional role, and what is secondary is kept so. Secondly there are those works dedicated to Corbu which are based on successful forms and idioms of the master (R.C. is Israel's basic material), and in the main these are skilled but diluted versions of their master's voice. Although successful in achieving a liveable atmosphere, their discipline is too limited for the architect to make major, original design decisions. Finally, there are those which are simply individualistic expressions of the architects themselves, avoiding the need to re-define problems with the programme in hand. It is difficult to see how this somewhat narrow path can contribute anything more valid than unique stylistic studies.

One does however feel that somewhere in all this there are forces at work that will shortly generate forms to give the expression and identity that this new nation is seeking.

Ram Karmi

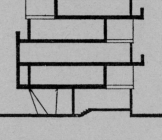

This 265-yard-long block forms one of the enclosing walls of the neighbourhood and contains about 200 flats of various sizes, facing east/west (the accepted wrong orientation) over carpet development.
In order to keep a limited number of entrances, balcony access is used, giving shade to the face of the building. To avoid long perspectives, these balconies are carried from one side of the block to the other at the vertical connections, which form joints with spaces where people may rest and talk; growth points to which future buildings may join; meeting places. Each section of balcony is either forty or eighty yards long and two storeys high, broken again into smaller sections by cells extended at the upper storey. This produces an unrepetitive elevation composed of large elements, each balcony section being on the opposite side of the building to those above, below, or next to it. Within each of these comprehensible numbers of large elements are a comprehensible number of cells, so that one can locate and identify one's own dwelling from the ground. This hierarchy of scale is also experienced in the materials, the outer skin being concrete, the surfaces along the access galleries brick, and within the cell plaster.
Each unit is itself entered off the access gallery, through a double-height courtyard, which is shaded — and more useful than the normal balcony on which one feels very exposed in Israel to the heat and glare. All major glass surfaces are thus able to be at right angles to the elevation and

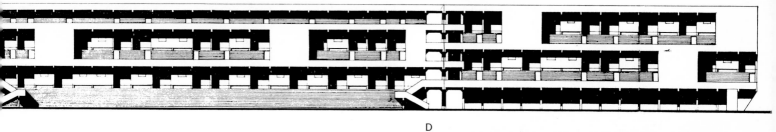

D

BEERSHEBA NEIGHBORHOOD

Architects

Yaski and Alexandroni, Karmi, Harkin, Zolotov

A

B

C

do not need the ubiquitous shutters. This solution of courtyards in the air prevents excessive overlooking of the carpet development beneath.

The fact that the elevations of this really very long building are composed of large-scale shade-giving circulation elements, and not louvred/structured façades, is symptomatic of a new searching for forms and relationships generated by the deeper probing of the specialness of functions involved, rather than the application of general formulae; a belief that a more accurate investigation of the specific does not mean an over-emphasis of certain attractive forms arising out of very minor functional requirements.

MASTER PLAN: *Below*

We tried to create a comprehensible unit by building a protective wall with carpet development inside, keeping open space to a minimum and creating as much shade as possible.

This wall is penetrated by a road which cuts through the enclosure diagonally, creating the centre where it passes under the main pedestrian link, the point of arrival and of departure.

You are either inside or outside the walls; you enter and leave through a kind of gateway; at the centre you change systems; you are aware always of the progressions of scale and your own position within them.

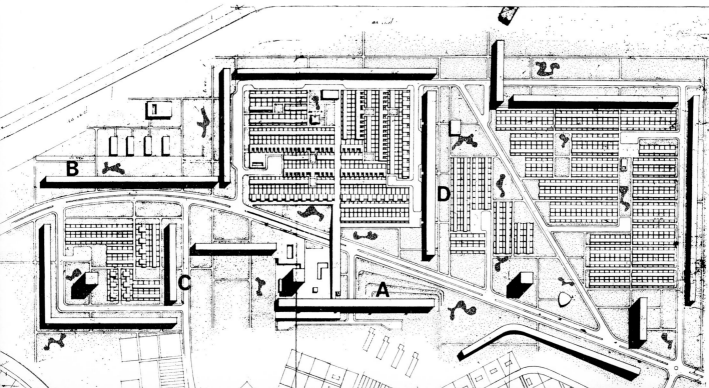

HOSTEL, NAZARETH

Architects

Yaski and Alexandroni

One-room bachelor flats (first floor) and three-room split-level family flats (second floor) have common access from a broad ambulatory on the 'blind' side. They are supported over an open ground floor on concrete pilotis. Communal rooms on the lower ground floor project so that their roof forms an entrance level terrace. The levels are built up in a section that knits closely into the slope of the hillside.

AFULA HOUSING

Architects

J. and O. Yahr

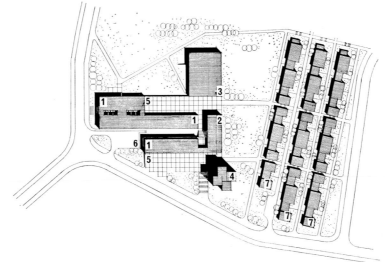

SITE PLAN KEY

1 Shopping centre
2 Library
3 Auditorium
4 Apartments
5 Terrace
6 Service road
7 Terrace houses

Upper Afula was planned fifteen years ago as an extension of Lower Afula on the slopes of the Israel Valley, across and along which it affords magnificent views. The streets run along the contours and are terraced alternately for pedestrians and vehicles, connected vertically by steps. The breaks in the terraces at first-floor level are staggered for the view. This simple street of houses is especially refreshing after passing through the sort of town planning described. Suddenly you find yourself in one meaningful street. The scale of the houses relates pleasantly to the whole, it is enclosed and shady, and despite the agency photographs, people stand and talk, and children play. If this is not a revolutionary solution, at least it works and you're glad to arrive in it.

GREECE

Contributing Editor

Orestis Doumanis

Typical modern classical revival in Athens

The rich architectural tradition of Greece has had a significant effect on the post-war work of her architects. However, as in other countries with an architectural heritage, misconceptions and the lure of the facile have restricted the influence of tradition to a mere imitation of morphological elements and details. Elements and forms of classical Greek architecture, the Byzantine churches and the popular architecture of the last two centuries are often repeated in contemporary buildings with fake materials, or in a modernized and stylized version. Even well-known architects and teachers have transposed elements from the past into their work, believing perhaps that they would thus preserve a period which was dear to them, and this eclecticism was often carried even further by their students. Perhaps this arose through the belief that in such a way a 'Greek school' of national architecture could be created. The Romantics, who have failed to be sensitive to the problems and demands of their own age, have created a substantial check to national architectural development.

Fortunately, there have been a few architects who have distinguished in the rich heritage of the past those elements and the spirit which must always, beyond time, constitute the characteristics of the country's architecture — simplicity and honesty in the use of materials and in construction, the inspiration of the landscape and a rational functionalism dictated by real needs.

The influence of contemporary international architecture, which was delayed for many years, is now evident, although the expression of the structure, the use of curtain walls and *brise-soleils*, etc., are frequently applied superficially and out of context. The influence of Mies van der Rohe and of Le Corbusier is also frequently found — although some examples — the result of a basic misconception — debase architecture into formalized design that aims simply to please a wealthy group of clients whose rise in living standards is not matched by any improvement in their cultural level. These examples are absurd exaggerations of superficial form, with an utter lack of visual understanding.

The authorities are unfamiliar with contemporary city-planning ideas,

New offices in Athens
Arch: N. Valsamakis

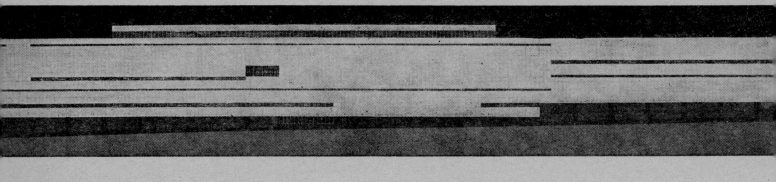

and the absence of master plans and state housing programmes has led to a monopoly of building by private organizations whose sole motivation is immediate, greater and easy profit. These organizations exploit the state's failure to create planning. The Greek housing problem is dealt with by indifferent solutions, and serious obstacles are placed in the path of future developments. Architects who are busy building apartment houses in the bigger towns do not have the opportunity to work without considering the profit motive and even assume the pecuniary mentality they are obliged to serve. In the case of small private houses, the absence of planning and the participation of speculators have led to the creation of huge amorphous housing projects, devoid of the most basic requirements where the prerequisites for the creation of architecture are non-existent.

The backwardness of the building industry in Greece has also had significant repercussions. This deficiency has arisen through the absence of a long-term housing programme which would have encouraged standardization and prefabrication, the indifference of private capital towards an industry which does not offer quick profits, and the low level of the country's technical development. There is a great need for a building industry that can provide architects with the possibility of satisfying present needs in a better way technically and financially, and finally to create better architecture.

State building is limited to the erection of a few public buildings entrusted to established architects, with mediocre results. There are few exceptions.

The overall picture of post-war Greek architecture is discouraging, even more so when compared to the work done in the first forty years of our century. But there are encouraging signs in the work of a few young, and even fewer older, architects who are alive to new directions in world architecture. Their buildings have a severe and sober appearance; a spirit of sobriety and simplicity that characterizes new architecture, devoid of the affectation and exhibitionism of the new baroque school that currently threatens to spread throughout the world. The enormity of contemporary problems urges these architects to look for new ways of construction to satisfy contemporary needs. Progress in technology, however slow, will make this satisfaction possible, and in time will achieve a better architecture and the creation of a better way of life.

Orestis Doumanis

Elevations of Fix Brewery, Athens
Arch: Takis Zenetos

Xenia hotel, Mykonos
Arch: A. Konstantinidis

House in Athens
Arch: A. Konstantinidis

National bank pavilion,
International Trade Fair, Salonica
Arch: N. Valsamakis

House in Athens
Arch: Takis Zenetos

FIX BREWERY, ATHENS

Architect

Takis Zenetos

A new beer factory is being constructed on the site of the old Fix brewery in Athens by the young architect Takis Zenetos. In common with his other work in Athens the project reveals his preoccupation with the means of achieving a dynamic architecture of growth and change.
The structure creates free space within the building and is separated from the cladding elements, which are arranged in an informal composition of solid and void to correspond to the internal planning.

Transparent glass and opaque insulating panels that are combined on the façades are hung on to a framework independent of the structure, and can be modified according to the changing needs of the production system.
The enormous length of the building with its emphatic horizontality contrasts vividly with the typically Athenian scatter of houses that surrounds the site. Huge glazed panels on the street elevation open up views into the interior with glimpses of large polished copper vats.

This apartment block develops the architect's idea of a dynamic architecture even further than the Fix brewery. The whole structure is a space-cage in which sliding panels of heat-resisting glass, windows, louvres and curtains are hung in receding planes. They are all interchangeable, produced industrially, and slide at a touch on channels and rollers; according to the prevailing weather (or to the idiosyncrasies of the occupier) they can provide total enclosure or can open up the interior as a completely windowless open space.

The architect rejects the solid masonry wall, rejects the static form of curtain walling, rejects the ubiquitous balcony.
The result is a building that is never the same: the chessboard theme of the façade is continually changing in dynamic patterns of light and shade.
At night, the artificial light is integrated with the system of sliding screens to reveal compositions in depth that dissolve the distinction between inside and outside: the façade is no longer a permanent and final operation.

APARTMENT HOUSE, ATHENS

Architect

Takis Zenetos

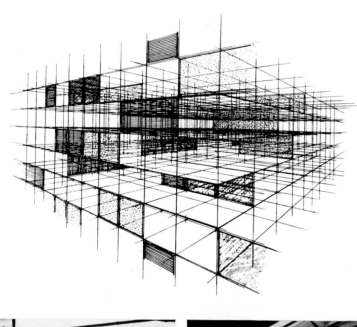

Bedroom block left, link centre,
restaurant and lounges right

XENIA MOTEL, KALAMBAKA

Architect

Aris Konstantinidis

*At the foot of the cliffs of Meteora
in central Greece, on the outskirts
of the small town of Kalambaka
and on the road leading to the
Italy ferry (Igomenitsa), the motel
has been built on the slope in such
a manner that all four storeys are
accessible from ground level. On
the lowest floor is the hall for the
cars; the two storeys above
accommodate 22 double rooms, each
with WC and shower. Located on
the main floor, the third, are the
drive-in, as a covered lobby with
reception office, service rooms, WC
and a small lounge, from which a
staircase leads up to the restaurant
on the fourth floor. The small
lounge is adorned by a relief, and
the seating area by the fireplace
in the restaurant with a sculpture
by K. Loukopoulos. In this
restaurant, the floor is of grey
marble, the fireplace of red brick.
The staircase connecting the three
lower storeys and the open corridor
in the room block have floors of red
cement tiles, iron frames and
panels of Novopan.*

Elevation of bedroom block

Link with bedroom block

Bedroom balconies

Vehicle access

Open gallery to bedrooms

Staircase hall to bedrooms

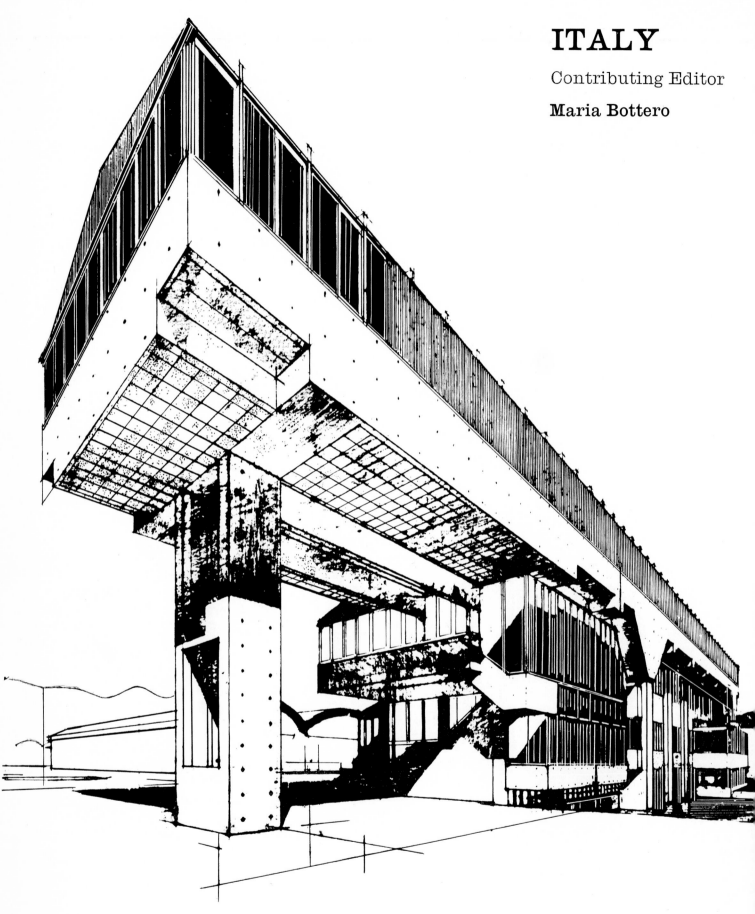

ITALY

Contributing Editor

Maria Bottero

The Crisis of a Culture

After the period of the fascist academy and the war, Italy emerged blasted by bombs and culturally backward; rebuilding and organization therefore had to be done in a new and modern way. In the immediate post-war years Italian architects rediscovered Frank Lloyd Wright and American organic architecture; they discussed pre-fabricated building, regional planning and reconstruction, problems of theory, aesthetics and design. It was an electrifying experience and one which was to lead to the fulfilment of many peoples' hopes. On a national scale provisions were made for regulating the methods of reconstructing urban centres, for increasing employment and for the creation of numerous institutes of popular building and the re-organization of the depressed areas in the south.

But the development of cities continued on its own account. Little more than ten years after the war, private property developers came on the scene to penetrate the loose mesh of the building regulations and reconstruction plans. They became an immense power, difficult to control, distorting the character and beauty of the traditional urban and natural landscapes, destroying, more than did the bombs, surroundings and monuments of historic interest, razing to the ground the green of the parks, and creating artificially rising values for areas capable of development. Some people set themselves the problem of finding barely adequate means to control speculation and limit its disastrous consequences.

A whole series of town-planning conventions on a national scale has been concerned with working out the most suitable methods of conserving urban and rural landscapes. It is not necessary to analyse these discussions here; it is only necessary to describe the cultural climate in which the Italian architecture of the last ten years has grown up.

The value of time, of history, and consequently the specific values of a culture have been rediscovered in contrast to the lucid abstractions of the best rationalism and its claim to cosmic and international qualities. The flexibility of empiricism is opposed to the exactitude of reason; the organic quality of free forms to geometrical perfection 'à l'esprit de géométrie l'esprit de finesse'.

The man for whom one is building is no longer an animal with standardized needs; he is a psychologically complex individual, firmly rooted in a clearly defined society, to whom it not only matters that the house runs perfectly, like a well-oiled machine, but also that it shall become an essential part of his world and have a sentimental and symbolic value.

The application with which Italian architects have studied empirical English and Scandinavian architecture is justified. Together with Wright's organic architecture it represents a revaluation of nature and of traditional building materials.

FACTORY, PORDENONE
Arch: Gino Valle

125

Town planning, to be really effective, must go hand-in-hand with economic planning and an effective legal system. It signifies nothing to single out an area if it is not conceived within the total sphere of influence of the city; while the city must be studied in relation to neighbouring cities, and in the light of regional interests. With more and more articulate and efficient methods of regional planning on a national scale, it is to be hoped that it will be possible to combat not only building speculation, but above all the serious lack of balance in the national economy, such as the concentration of industry in the north opposed to the agricultural economy and backwardness of the south. Milan is perhaps the most eloquent symbol of this lack of balance; the futuristic city of glass walls and speculative demolition by which the historic and nineteenth century centre will be virtually obliterated; of continual immigration, whirling growth, rapid dissolution and indiscriminate renewal. Here, more than anywhere else, industry imposes the rhythm of mass-production and determines the consumer's market, creating the neo-capitalist economy of modern industry as an agonizing alternative to the agricultural and pre-industrial economy of the south.

The vastly complex means of planning and intervention poses the grave problem of how to define the work of the architect: in what manner and towards what goal it must be directed, and at what point in this continual stratification of operations it should be introduced. Such a complex differentiation means re-evaluating not only the architect's profession, but also, generally speaking, the significance of his art, the role of technology and the validity of formal idiom. The argument extends until it questions the suggestion that architecture can be today what it has always been in the past: an idiomatic and stylistic operation which synthesizes, in the particular and proper meaning of the expression, every formal and technological innovation.

The Present Crisis

A state of crisis in art and architecture could be said to exist, a crisis evident at two levels: within the town planning and politico-economic structure in which the architect works, and within the architect's own style and personal modes of expression. What are the symptoms of crisis in this double situation?

From the political and objective point of view, from the immediate post-war period to the present day, it is already obvious that the predominant element in the development of building and town planning has been disorder; the part played by architects has been more or less inferior, indulgent towards old mannerisms, and incapable of any positive influence on the building trade which, in the congested production of the whole post-war period, has been almost entirely governed by commercial and speculative interests. This state of affairs obviously gets worse as time goes on.

Crisis is not too strong a word: crisis in town planning and building; crisis, too, in the idiom of personal expression. And as there are essentially two levels on which the crisis of a culture can be perceived, there are also two ways in which the younger generation of architects can consciously combat the crisis. One approach is typified by the so-called revivalist works which follow diverse and often very unexpected patterns of stylistic inspiration, a renewal of idiom over and above the canons of between-wars rationalism. In this trend the necessity for renewal is seen essentially in relation to the idiomatic structures, in which intolerance of conformity shows itself in the rejection of current formulae, and the frequent and unjustifiable substitution of stylistic elements from the past.

The alternative solution is proposed by the technicians. They consider that many significant achievements easily degenerate into the personal and obscure; they propose restrictive legislation in town-planning matters, a fair political system for each area, and finally a collective effort to define and state effective methods of achieving economic and urban planning which will include the entire national, inter-

THE RINASCENTE
Archs: Albini and Helg

OLIVETTI COMMUNITY CENTRE
Arch: Gardella

FACTORY, PORDENONE
Arch: Gino Valle

connected territory. Naturally the division between revivalists and technicians is not so precise, nor are the programmes of the two groups so explicit.

A vaguely uneasy feeling is evident in this delineation of pure form and pure technique. But do pure form and pure technique really exist, and are they indeed realizable? The crisis manifests itself by attacks from time to time on one or other of these two standpoints. Is this not already a symptom of the crisis? In fact, the formalists and rationalists are not so very far from one another. Programmes which freely evolve from each persuasion tend to overlap in the end. The complicated technical, productive and idiomatic processes of society cannot be forcibly simplified and schematically reduced to a single one of its arguments.

The insufficiency and danger of these attitudes bring about operative aridity, and an inflexible systematization of the expressive idiom through a false clarity and over-simplification of the real problems; while the positive examples deliberately aim at clarity of communication and a real extension of the semantic area of the idiom.

The three works which we present come from architects of very different natures. Franco Albini and Ignazio Gardella are two Milanese architects of international repute who were both moulded in the school of the best Italian rationalism, but they have very different temperaments. Gino Valle is a young architect from Udine, who took his degree at the Venetian school and afterwards, in the U.S.A., getting the opportunity to study at close quarters the work of Mies, Wright, Kahn and younger American architects such as Rudolph.

In spite of the differences of temperament and culture in their authors, these three works approach each other closely. They propose, from a very diverse idiomatic selection, a searching after real expressive possibilities, not confined to an artificially simplified vision of present reality; even if the search gets into deep water, it is with enough precise knowledge to remain afloat.

This seems to be the case with Albini, in whom it is not difficult to discern beyond the rigorous morality of a typically Lombard nature the reflected image of morality, the moral of morality, if one may so put it, in a play of parallel mirrors reaching out through space toward the mystery of the infinite. It would not be mistaken, in this context, to talk of his religious and divine sentiment. His architecture is the exact transposition in stylistic terms of the tormented image and reflection of this sentiment. Everyone knows his famous settings for exhibitions, where space is traversed by wires and transparent planes, picked out in luminous points and swept by ribbing and forceful lines; space which is no longer physically concrete, but a metaphysical network where even pillars and supports become graphic signs of great elegance. Albini is rightly considered to be one of the best Italian designers. Always present in him is the necessity to industrialize and serialize the object; but combined with this necessity is the knowledge that the duty of the designer is to resist the lowering of standards prompted by fashion and the pressures of the market. Therefore his objects are never obvious; they do not even have the natural quality which comes of a true relationship between form and function. On the contrary, they are extremely complicated, they are true machines in which even the smallest cog finds its proper place in the system; this is further complicated by his desire to exhibit the whole mechanism, with all the most secret wheels that make it work, in order to demonstrate the beauty of technology and the rigour of form.

Gardella is of a very different temperament to Albini. His attitude towards different problems has always been one of empirical conciliation; and if his architecture, like Albini's, can be defined as typically Lombard and Milanese, it is not on account of a severe morality so much as the technological rigourousness which shapes it, and above all in its being essentially an architecture that depends wholly on glazes and chromatic transparencies, like the best painting and architecture of Lombardy.

The empiricism of Gardella is rooted in the experience he gained as a young man of Northern and Finnish architecture, which he soon proffered as an alternative (more adapted to his temperament) to the canons of rationalism. It is not by chance that his work has been evaluated and discovered in post-war years, when Italian culture, having discovered American organic architecture, again turned its attention to the empiricism of northern Europe. The influx of decorative and traditional elements into the idiom is no novelty to Gardella; they naturally make up a part of his intelligent awareness of the traditional and specific values of a culture. Decoration has assumed a special significance; it seems to him one of the most valid and sure ways of escaping from a critical situation where idiom is concerned, in the attempt to make this more expressive and pregnant, loaded with allusions to a tradition or to a particular region. Thus Gardella means to imply that the duty of the architect is to concentrate his own forces on the elaboration of the idiomatic structure, rather than to dedicate himself, as the technologists want to do, to the re-organization of industry and the economic and political structure of the country. For, says Gardella, reforms of that sort are only possible outside the sphere of architecture, through responsible political initiative; to claim the ability to solve such huge problems in the architect's studio would be like '. . . wanting to make nuclear experiments in a bicycle shop'. It might seem that in his attempt at evaluation of idiom Gardella falls back on revivalism, but in reality one should see in this position the flowering of an exquisitely empirical and tactical nature, ready to recognize the limits of intervention and within these limits to solve the problem in the best way possible.

A great distance (due to the difference in age, formation and cultural outlook) separates Gino Valle from Albini and Gardella. It seems that this formally bold and confident architecture annuls the significance of every controversy about idiom, expression, harmony with existing surroundings, the collaboration of the architect with industry and the introduction of individual work into a predetermined social structure. This is probably due to the fact that these problems are felt less at Milan than elsewhere, and, moreover, that Valle appreciated them, not just through provincial isolation, but through the means of a far-reaching cultural formation, which extends from the experience of modern American architecture (Gino Valle studied at the Harvard Graduate Center under Gropius) to a close study of Le Corbusier, and above all of Aalto. Also the Venice school of architecture (where Valle took his degree) probably contributed to a cultural foundation of this sort, as an overture to his international experience.

Apart from this opening to a tradition wider than the regional one, the experimental and unbiased attitude from which a form grows plays a most important role in Valle's architecture, from the most logical and rational solution to a problem, from the use of the appropriate materials, to reliable technical procedure. For Valle there is no *a priori* problem of existing surroundings, or at least it is no more than one of many factors that condition the projection of a work, and is defined in the project itself.

The gulf is evident between this kind of position and that of Gardella, for example. Gardella reconciles rigorous technique with frankly decorative exigencies of style, which justify themselves in sentimental attachment to the splendours of the bourgeois tradition of the nineteenth century, or in the fascination that a special atmosphere like that of Venice can exert on him. Valle feels no necessity for sentimental accord with a place or a tradition; if the necessity arises, it is only in the functional or critical terms by which any object is defined in a precise historical or social situation.

The technical correctness and precision of Valle's work never rises to the plane of romance or myth, as happens with Albini, where it becomes an emotive pretext and enters into architectural composition as an element of fantasy. Technology for Valle is a means in itself, without any reserve of sentiment. His lack of prejudice with regard to technology and his willingness to collaborate with industry mark him as a classic designer, artist and cultivated man, whose work is introduced directly into the system of industrial production. This is why Valle finds himself outside the current controversies without being open to accusations either of formalism or of empty technological exhibitionism, and certainly not of ignorance of present problems.

Maria Bottero

THE RINASCENTE, GENOA

Architects

Franco Albini and Franca Helg

The Rinascente is one of Albini's latest works, in which he collaborated with the architect Franca Helg. As in the municipal office building at Genoa, or in organized architectonics of town-planning in the Piccapietra quarter of Genoa, one can sense the effort of striving to harmonize with the surroundings. The accentuation of the projecting bays of the structure in horizontal steel, and the sharp and lively contrast of colours between the facing of pink slabs and the dark grey ironwork, the corrugations of the facings and the decorative courses of white *graniglia*, show that the architect wanted to make a simple statement, rich in descriptive elements reflecting the influence of the surroundings, and also those derived from the theme itself (references to the big nineteenth-century cast-iron buildings are quite explicit). These elements intend, above all, to make the idiom clearer, and therefore more communicative. The projecting bays that contain the services, the exterior corrugated surfaces of *graniglia* made to contain the vertical ducts, are strictly functional as well as decorative: they verify the complexity and strength of a work by Albini in which technological, expressive and idiomatic researches are all founded on a choice of style.

Photos: Oscar Savio

THE RINASCENTE
Pre-cast concrete and steelwork
detailing

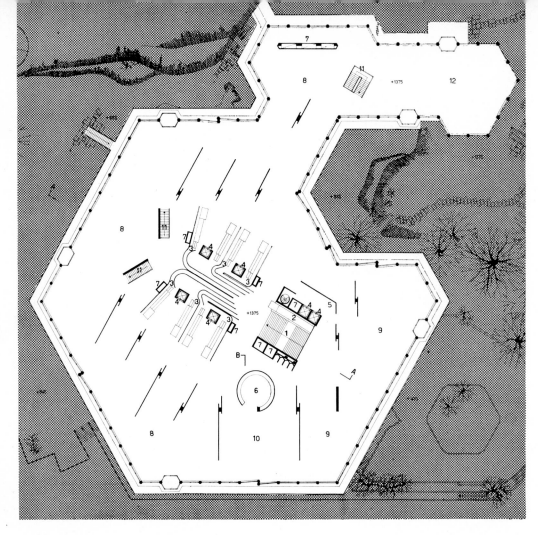

OLIVETTI COMMUNITY HALL, IVREA

Architect

Ignazio Gardella

The Olivetti community hall at Ivrea represents one of the most important of Gardella's works, in which can be seen all the specific qualities that characterize his designs. Built on a relatively small area, and shut in between the main Olivetti factory and the hill, it adapts itself to the surroundings in a simple and natural way, exploiting the space at its disposal, as well as the different ground-levels and the existing trees. The plan in the form of an open hexagon; the almost total use of glass for the external fittings; the snaking of the continuous line of balconies along all sides of the building, which accentuates the effect of growing out along the horizontal dimension; the railings of the balconies which, together with the glass-covered walls, confer lightness and transparency — all these things can be defined as classic elements of Gardella's style, made up of chromatic surfaces and transparencies. Inside the building, air-conditioning ducts run up to the ceiling like vegetable growths, surfaces of black and white designs (in white marble and slate) along the stairs and the parapets of the balconies, confirm Gardella's desire to explore the possibilities of decoration; if, in some cases such as the air-conditioning ducts, it exploits the functional elements of construction, elsewhere it is an end in itself, faithful to its proper capacity to suggest new expressive possibilities.

Photos: Casali

Photos: Publifoto

OLIVETTI COMMUNITY HALL
Interiors

Photo: Italo Zannier

FACTORY FOR ZANUSSI AND REX, PORDENONE

Architect

Gino Valle

The building for the works of Zanussi and Rex at Pordenone is an example of the high level reached in Valle's architecture. Situated on the Pontebana national highway, on a plain enclosed by a range of mountains on the horizon, the building extends like a barricade transversely to a group of hangars housing the works, a kind of bridge commanding the entrance, under which one has to pass in order to enter the works. The whole building is rather like a ship, long and narrow, with a regular rhythm of windows and projections. The treatment of the reinforced concrete exterior shows as a regular pattern of sharp corners through the use of metal formwork. The structure is composed of a series of double frames set transversely to the building and supporting the storeys which jut out on the north side and (the top storey) on the south side. These ceiling-balconies, stepped down on the north side, all have a reinforced concrete parapet on which is hung the metal structure of the windows.

The result is an architecture plastically and emotionally rich, but it is also as precise as a machine, and absolutely free from descriptive decoration. On the other hand its expressive power, the style of formal severeness and austerity it displays, reduces form to structure and structure to form, stabilizing between these two terminals a mathematical equation. In this difficult, but not impossible, equilibrium lies the expressive potential of a new architecture.

PLAN

SECTION

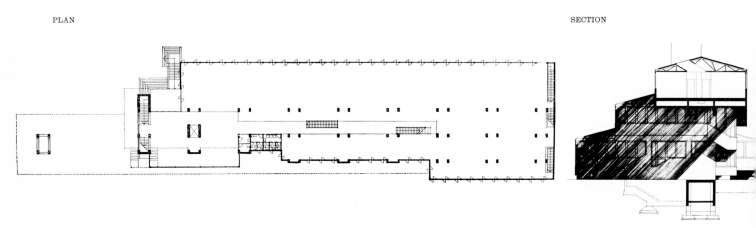

136

LONG SECTION

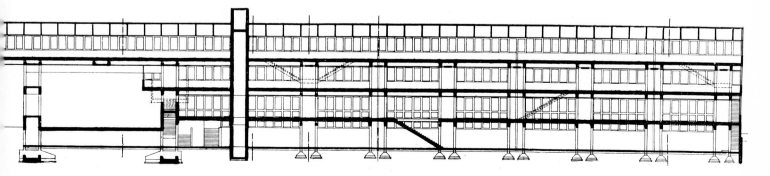

Photos: Italo Zannier

POLAND

Contributing Editor

Oskar Hansen

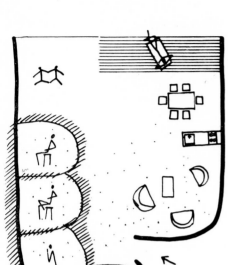

Open Form and the Greater Number

The main problem in our architecture is the identity of the individual within the 'Greater Number':

> How to shape space in the form of innumerable cells, each of them containing, not — as those of a honeycomb — a bee, but a human individual.

An attempt at solving this deadlock between quantity and quality is the proposed system which I call *Open Form*. This system changes the content of architecture as so far conceived. It establishes two formative factors: an objective one — where the community is the acting force, and a subjective one — the domain of the individual. The first factor shapes the raw construction of residential schemes, technical equipment, communications and social facilities — all that is inherent in the privilege of belonging to the community; while the second is that in which the individual moulds his immediate environment. This releases the resources latent in the 'Great Number', so far treated as passive, and thus to some extent relieves the first factor.

The Open Form system leads to a qualitative change: to the appreciation of personality in the community, of the *individual in the Great Number*. The architecture of Open Form will find expression in a system of development, not just a grouping of 'tenements', resulting from a coherent mingling of objective (collective) with subjective (individual) elements. When these subjective elements of environment are co-ordinated with the objective elements of construction the result is the *Art of Spontaneous Occurrence*.

The purpose of the aesthetics of Open Form is to communicate the rich, organic polemics of *Occurring Forms*. This is achieved through enlarging the sphere of action of subjective phenomena, not by the elimination of particular forms (as in the aesthetics of Closed Form) but by consideration of particular component elements.

Excerpt from a paper read at the Lublin Conference of the Association of Polish Architects

HOUSING FOR GROWTH AND CHANGE
Archs: Lukasiewicz and Pinno

Above:
Analysis of the needs for space and light within the apartment.

Below:
FLEXIBILITY OF THE VOLUME
The adopted system of flat layouts makes it possible to apply various depths and widths of buildings ranging from forty to a hundred feet and to design flats of different and changing sizes.

The theory of Open Form has been known in Poland since 1956. Designs containing some features of Open Form appear from time to time, particularly among the younger generation, in opposition to the dull uniformity of housing design. Two of these projects, little known so far are presented here.

Oskar Hansen

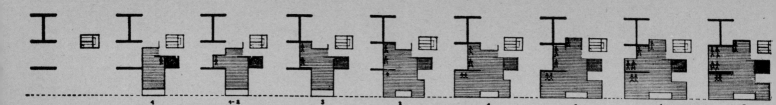

HOUSING FOR GROWTH AND CHANGE

Architects

Lukasiewicz and Pinno

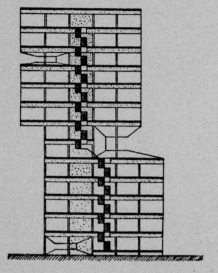

Flexibility of the section

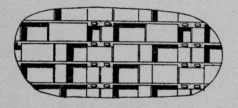

Flexibility of the elevation

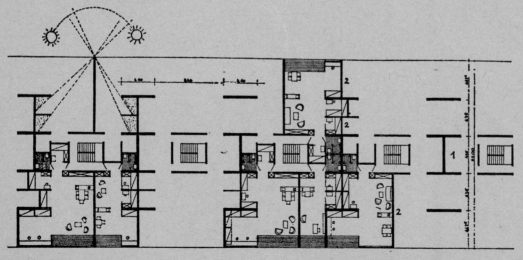

Flexibility of individual plans

As a result of an analysis of the functions of particular rooms, and of their requirements with respect to sunlighting, external space and ventilation, the designers adopted the principle of shaping the flat in the depth of the building, perpendicularly to the elevation. The rooms that have the most sunlight are the children's room and the living-room. The bathroom and WC have no sunlight at all.

The living room has the maximum area possible under the economic conditions of the moment. The need to give each person a room (sanctuary) of his own, however small, was considered so important that the team decided to design individual cubicles, which are properly air-conditioned.

Both these spaces penetrate into each other. The sound-proof sliding walls of the cubicles make it possible to incorporate them into the general area of the flat. So the whole flat is mobile and flexible, and the living room may be enlarged for such purposes as entertaining visitors or day activities of the entire family. By shutting himself in his sanctuary, on the other hand, each member of the family may isolate himself at night, or when he wishes to work or relax.

Horizontal communications within the building take the form of streets provided every six floors. The main street on the sixth floor, where the basic service facilities are accommodated, is at the same time a corso — a recreation space for the inhabitants of the building. Its spatial and functional design promotes community life. Access from the streets to particular flats is by local staircases, while connection with the ground level is provided by a system of lifts.

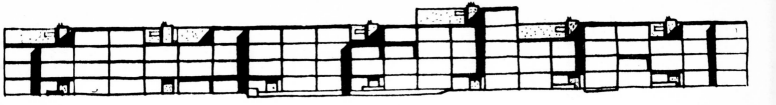

SETTLEMENT FOR 15,000, PTOCK

Architects

Grebecka and Kobylanski

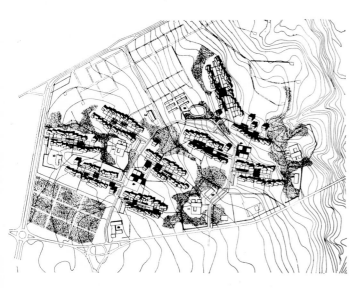

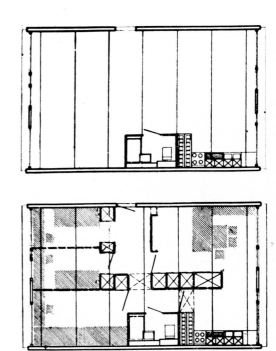

The urban pattern of this settlement is hinged on the premise that the flat is the basic cell in both functional and plastic composition.

These flats form chains of different height — from three to five storeys — and have spread into the green areas destined for the recreation of the inhabitants. But as they are densely built along converging streets it has been possible to surround the whole scheme with a fairly large green area, and at the same time achieve an overall density of 240 people per acre.

The green areas contain schools and playgrounds for the children as well as recreation areas for adults. The two shopping centres are in the residential streets. The architects, in an attempt to give a certain individuality to the flats, decided to adopt an open-plan system, where only the main construction walls and sanitary equipment were mass produced; the inhabitants are easily able to lay out and erect pre-fabricated partitions which allow for future change.

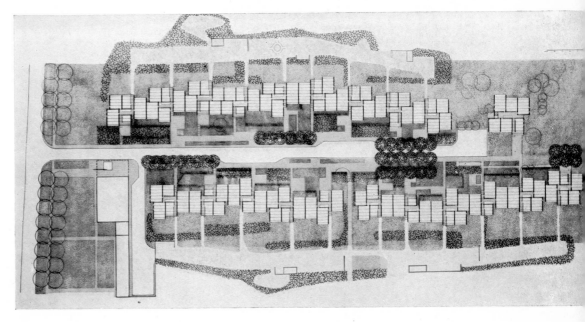

143

THE START SPORTS CENTRE, WARSAW

Architects

Ihnatowicz, Soltan, Tomaszewski, Gessler and Wittek

Photos: Kupuscik

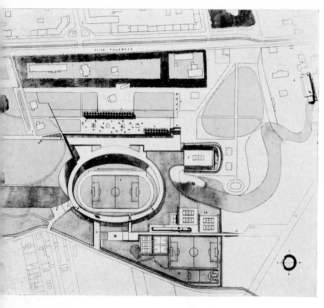

The Sports Centre is situated on an escarpment, approximately sixty-five feet high, which crosses the city from north to south. West of the escarpment, and running parallel to it, is an important traffic artery which provides the main access to the Sports Centre. Between this artery and the Centre a tree-planted protective zone has been designed, which at the same time integrates the existing scanty development.

Towards the east the site slopes down, opening up a deep view over the wide valley of the Vistula. The basic idea of the design consists in moulding the site into four terraces as follows:

(a) on the first terrace — training facilities;

(b) on the second terrace — the main stadium with grandstands seating about 7,000 spectators;

(c) the third terrace is laid out in the form of a corso which provides access to the grandstand of the stadium. This corso is usually available to the public and forms part of the system of pedestrian walks along the escarpment. An arena for small games — tennis, hockey and volley-ball — with seats for 2,000 spectators has been designed on the same terrace;

(d) the fourth, uppermost terrace is to be an open-air swimming-pool. All the buildings are made of simple weather-proof materials requiring a minimum of maintenance, i.e. raw concrete, rolled steel, timber, lime brick and glass.

The terraces have been shaped with the help of earth escarpments and retaining walls. The latter are designed on the principle of a 'biological' reinforcement of earth masses with pre-fabricated concrete units. This method has made it possible to achieve considerable savings on concrete (approximately 40%) and to obtain interesting aesthetic effects.

HUNGARY

Contributing Editor

Charles Polónyi

Iparterv, Budapest

Designing and planning bureau of
industrial and agricultural buildings

PLANT FOR THE TISZA CHEMICAL COMBINE

Architect

László Bajnay

The Hungarian chemical industry's development plan scheduled the establishment of the 'TISZA' Chemical Combine, comprising a series of producing groups. The nitrous fertilizer plant had been erected in the initial building period, and was to be followed by other plants, in the first instance for the production of plastics.

The fertilizer plant comprises twenty different factories, the office and the social-building, with a total volume of 1,177,160 cubic yards. The plants belonging to later building periods are scheduled with similar dimensions. The client did not wish to interfere with the planning, expecting only designing and erecting methods which considered the characteristics of the site, the capacity of the Hungarian building industry and the shortest processes of erection.

Considering the available means, the designers started by standardizing the structural system. Economic and technical reasons necessitated reinforced concrete structures in the major part, the building enterprise having acquired wide experience with prefabricated elements. A further advantage of prefabrication is that the construction continues in winter, needs less skilled workers and achieves improved quality. A prefabrication plant erected at the site produces a series of components in large quantities, with relatively small investment. By dimensional standardization we obtained the effective factor of production, i.e. large quantities of few types.

According to the lay-out, a basic module of twenty-three inches appeared to meet all requirements.

The basic module — applied in three dimensions — determined in the first instance the major load-bearing and walling structures. The enterprise which furnished the mechanical equipment for the prefabrication appreciated our aims and has a due claim to their success.

With the introduction of dimensional standardization we obtained the following advantages:

> reduction of factory-types, and standardization of the space-function needs of each type;
> decrease of the types of prefabricated elements, so that the principle of interchangeability becomes realizable;
> simplification of building methods and standardization of equipment — thus, economy in the designing process;
> standardization of building equipment (lifting and conveying devices) with adaptation of related processes;
> the possibility of future technological modifications without involving major structural alterations.

A detailed co-ordination of dimensional standardization was the basic preliminary and the most important feature for the selection of the elements. We adopted the simple method of 'addition', and assembled buildings for different functions with identical elements.

Photos: János Bognár

PIER HOTEL ON LAKE BALATON

Architect

Charles Polónyi

Is a strand-hotel at the pier more valuable than a similar one built elsewhere? The question had to be asked, and as a result a site was chosen between the beach and the pier. The small area available and the views, equally fine in every direction, made it necessary to have a rather high structure on a circular ground-plan.

The kitchen, restaurant and social rooms are in a horizontal slab which meets the cylindrical tower at its base, as they cannot reasonably fit into the homogeneous, circular system.

The horizontal section is partially open and merges with the ground between beach and pier. By covering this section we obtain open lobbies, an entrance to the strand and also to the restaurant on the upper floor — which is reached directly by a second stair facing the pier. The upper floor houses the kitchen, a lobby and a social room, which is also used for cinema performances, lectures, etc., before and after the bathing season.

The vertical hotel part supports a roof-garden extension of the restaurant on the pier side. On the shore side there is a separate roof for residents, arranged for games and sunbathing, and including resting enclosures. There is an adjacent saloon-bar, separated by convenient acoustic insulation.

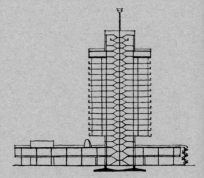

PHARMACEUTICAL PLANT, DEBRECEN

Photos: János Bognár

Architects

Zoltán Gulyás and Jenö Szendröi

In the woods surrounding Debrecen, one of the largest cities on the Great Hungarian Plain, we have started to construct this plant for the final treatment of pharmaceutical products. Basic materials arrive from different factories; this plant serves only for final processing and packaging.

The vertical spatial formation of towers is designed to waste as little green space as possible and to provide a more efficient and economic mechanical transportation, circulation and handling system than would be possible with a horizontal arrangement. Construction will proceed in three distinct stages, each comprising two units of laboratories twelve storeys high linked to a higher service and storage tower. Each stage is functionally and compositionally self-contained. On completion of the final group the three service and storage towers will combine to form an integrated central composition. Pedestrians and traffic enter the buildings on different levels.

Construction is of reinforced concrete frames, with lattice steel floors, which house all laboratory services. The blind walls of the storage towers will be of reinforced concrete, erected with a system of sliding shutters.

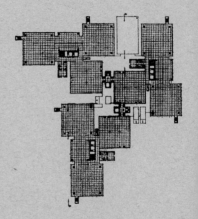

148

FRANCE

Contributing Editor

Shadrach Woods

Photo: Yan

Urban Environment
The Search For System

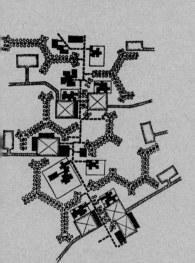

TOULOUSE-LE-MIRAIL

In order to consider the problems facing architects and planners today, it is necessary to eliminate such words as architecture, town-planning, urbanism. All these have meanings held over from previous civilizations and societies; meanings good or bad; in any case, meanings which do nothing but obscure the issues today. We are concerned, not with 'architecture' or 'town planning', but with the creation of environment for every scale of human association.

One hears it said fairly often, for instance: 'This building is not Architecture', or 'We must attack this problem as Architects, for that is what we are.' Clearly these statements refer to some previous context where Architecture was a *quality* to be conferred on 'good' buildings, not a *fact*, as it is today; or when Architects had only one way of thinking about problems, which means that their field of creativity was voluntarily restricted, not expanded, as it must be today.

The problems which we face in making our world are entirely new, for our society is entirely new; indeed our perception of the universe we live in is completely different from that of previous periods. The realization, for instance, that 'the scene of action of reality is not a three-dimensional Euclidean space but rather a four-dimensional world in which space and time are linked together indissolubly'[1] sets our civilization apart from any others.

The concept of society towards which we strive: that of a completely open, non-hierarchic co-operative in which all share on a basis of total participation and complete confidence, is not new, but we have covered so great a distance towards this goal that our position in relation to it is, perhaps for the first time, more realist than idealist. We are nearly there: 'It is good to know that a Utopia is never anything but the reality of tomorrow.'[2]

The facts of our physical and social milieu condition our attitudes toward design. We cannot seriously think of buildings as symbols of authority in a world where the very concept of authority is in question. We cannot think of planning in static terms, in three-dimensional space, when we live in a four-dimensional world.

Our primary concern is neither the making of objects in space nor yet the enclosure of spaces (however significant). It is the organization of places

(1) Herman Weyl *Raum Zeit Materie* 1921
(2) Le Corbusier *Le Modulor* 1948

and ways for the carrying out of human activities in our time. The creation of environment, our responsibility, begins with a way of thinking about organization in a given place at a given time, is realized in the discovery of a system of relationships and, finally, achieves plastic expression. The entire process has as its object the integration of specific activities into the total social, economic, technological context. The end is functional, in the same way that all art must be: it illuminates a society and prepares it for the next step along the way of man's progress. The plastic manifestation is not incidental to this process. It is of primary importance, remaining as the only evidence of intention; but it would be meaningless out of its organizational or sociological context.

As long as societies were evolving within the limits of simple hierarchic human groupings (tribes, villages, towns, classes, castes and sects), so long could design operate within the limits of purely visual disciplines. With the break away from these hierarchies, as society tends to become universal, the need for a new system is clearly felt.

The 'visual group' and its disciplines continue to operate but, alone, are no longer adequate to express the scale of human relationships today. New systems beyond the visual are required to illuminate those relationships. In the same way that we have broken out of Euclidean space in mathematics and physics through the apprehending of the fourth dimension, we must call upon the entire range of sense, intellect and emotion to create environment which corresponds to our aspirations towards a total society.

Today space is total and society is universal. The world of space and time is continuous. These realities must be reflected in our design and in our buildings.

The rediscovery of continuous total space, as opposed to discontinuous contained space, is the most important contribution of plastic art to twentieth-century society. The demonstration is made: the world is one, a continuous surface, surrounded by continuous space. The consequences of this demonstration are beginning to be felt: no longer can individuals or authorities appropriate portions of that space for their use exclusively. Continuity in space engenders continuity in society. Total space and universal society are interdependent. The one cannot exist without the other, and the existence of each guarantees the development of the other.

To incorporate the realities of total space and universal society into the creation of environment, to deal with these problems of space and society on today's scale, we set up systems (intellectual disciplines) which can relate activities and can be understood. The understanding must come through the perception of the parts of the system, since the whole can never be comprehended. We seek to discover processes which will lead us to the realization of our continuous society as surely as certain visual groups gave clear expression to the compartmented societies which they served. In this search for a way to attack the problem of environmental design, it is clear that we shall have to dispense with the use of symbols and monuments, for our society has no need of these crutches of authority. The authority of a universal society, if it can be said to exist, is not imposed through formalism or allegories. This is a fact which none oppose.

Stem

As it became clear that visual disciplines and compositional techniques alone were no longer adequate to the problem of creating an environment for our society, we looked for other ways to approach the problem. We began by considering two families of components: Dwellings and Ancillaries. This process may be compared to the concept of design by dissociation, which has long been general practice in the organization of housing units. A core is first determined by abstracting from the programme those elements which are easily defined (entry, kitchen, stairs, bath, etc.), then the rooms are clustered around these services. Servant and served, as Louis Kahn puts it, are defined and the core brings clarity and organization to the cluster.

TOULOUSE-LE-MIRAIL

TOULOUSE-LE-MIRAIL

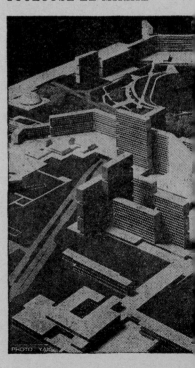

Photo: Yan

Using this same reasoning, we felt urban design could be considered as proceeding from stem to quarter or city, and that a basic structure could be determined, including all the servants of dwellings, all the *prolongements du logis*: commercial, cultural, educational and leisure activities, as well as roads, footpaths and services.

These are the Ancillaries, which vary from one place to another and from year to year. If they are taken as determinants of a scheme, they can, through the discovery of the relationships between them, give it clarity, organization and identity of a higher order than that which can be obtained solely from plastic or spatial arrangements.

Stem, then, is considered not as a simple linking mechanism between additive cells but as a generator of habitat. It provides the environment in which the cells function. It was evident that in taking this approach to environmental design, in concentrating on a basic structure, we could incorporate into that structure the characteristics of mobility and growth and change, which would then necessarily affect the whole complex, both cells and structure.

We tried to discover the relationships between human activities, and how these can be used to organize our dwellings, ways and places. Organize is used here in the sense of becoming organic. And since there is no life without change, we sought to use this principle and to make change, or at least the possibility of change, one of the basic conditions of design.

The obvious approach was, of course, a linear organization. A line is open-ended; it has no dimension; it can change direction at will. When we organize human activities and habitat into a linear system, the line becomes a Stem to which dwellings attach themselves.

We sought to reconcile the scales of speed of the automobile and the pedestrian and found that these scales are, in geometric terms, not supplementary but complementary, not parallel but perpendicular. They can only meet at points, never in lines.

When we apply this principle to our linear association of activities, which has become a Stem, we determine points along the stem where private transport can have access. The determination of these points where the automobile stops gives us logical places of entry into the dwelling complex. These are the points at which the different scales of speed meet, the places where the motorist becomes a pedestrian and where the pedestrian can, if he wishes, become a motorist. But the Stem remains a pedestrian way — a street, not a road.

Photo: Yan

Web

After having explored some of the possibilities of a system approach to environmental design, and having shown that Stem was indeed a valid tool for the organizing of urban environment, we are now exploring the directions which our search has opened to us. If we consider circulation, whether it be mechanical or pedestrian, it is evident that the idea of continuity in the system is essential. Indeed, continuity in the whole organization, so that no parts of it are in danger of isolation and none subject to an *a priori* over-densification, is absolutely basic for an evolving society. Chains of relationships and circulations are continuous, cyclical, and therefore tend towards the infinite. There is no beginning or end to the system, just as there is no centre as opposed to non-centre.

When we predetermine points of maximum intensity — centres — we are fixing a present or projected state of activities and relationships. We are perpetuating an environment where some places are central and others not, without, however, any competence for determining which things belong in which places. We compromise the future, closing doors instead of opening them.

> A point is static, fixed.
> A line is a measure of liberty.
> A non-centric web [3] is a fuller measure.

(3) This word is used to designate Stem to the next degree, Stem squared, as it were.

Within the discipline of a continuous system we may achieve a certain liberty in the articulation of function. Indeed it is only within some total order that function may become articulate. The parts of a system take their identity from the system. If there is no system, or order, there can be no identity but only a chaos of disparate entities engaged in pointless competition.

The purpose of any synthesis — to create a whole which is greater than the sum of the parts — can only be achieved if we can guarantee a total order comprising all the functions.

It is ridiculous and puerile to seek out the forms and techniques of the past, for their validity has gone with their society and can never return.

In the search for systems we first try to discover the conditions governing systems. Among those conditions which we assume as essential, are (in no special order):

The systems will be such that man can, within them, contribute to the creation of his environment, and, in so doing, ameliorate the total environment. This condition holds at all levels, from man in general to each particular man. It is the main reason for the systems.

The systems will have more than the three Euclidean dimensions. They will necessarily include the time dimension.

The systems will be sufficiently flexible to permit and encourage growth and change within themselves throughout the course of their lives. This is the true organic principle.

The systems will remain open, both in respect to smaller systems within them and in respect to greater systems around them. Smaller systems must be able to connect to them freely and they themselves must be able to connect freely to greater systems.

The systems will present, in their conception, an even intensity throughout. In order not to compromise the future, they will not establish, by their nature, any hierarchy of density or intensity of activity.

The character and possibly the extent of the systems will be apparent, or at least ascertainable, from the perception of their parts.

All these conditions can help us to find a way to approach the search for systems and, thence, to a true poetic discovery of the art of creating environment.

Web is not primarily a circulation system but an environmental one. It is a way to establish a large-scale order which, by its nature, makes possible individual expression on a smaller scale within a total context.

Web is a highly flexible system in a rapidly changing world. On the scales at which we are required to operate today, treating of the environment of tens or of hundreds of thousands, it is not possible to conceive of long-range plans being based on any fixed spatial or compositional relationships. Even as the first part of a plan is realized, it changes the conditions which govern the next stage, and, by continuous feedback, the whole plan. The non-centric, open-ended Web will respond to this life process.

The openness of the system is guaranteed by establishing an even intensity of activities over the Web, so that it can be 'plugged-into' at any point and can itself connect to greater systems from any point. The connections, of course, provoke points of greater intensity as they are made, but the original flexibility always remains, and the peaks of intensity which occur as the Web becomes poly-centric through use will retain a non-fixed character.

Web is intended to find ways of circulation by which men on foot can exist and associate without inflicting hardship on men in machines. It will therefore re-establish the human scale in urban design.

Shadrach Woods

Rejected entry of a plan for BILBAO. *Archs:* Candilis, Josic and Woods.

KEY
1 Centre
2 Dwellings
3 Sports
4 Industry
5 Airport
6 Port
7 Metro

BOCHUM UNIVERSITY PROJECT. *Archs:* Candilis, Josic and Woods.
Rejected competition scheme for projected Ruhr University. The programme called for a complete University including the Liberal Arts and Sciences and a teaching hospital of 2,800 beds. Ten thousand students were to be accommodated in hostels which together with sports fields were to be integrated in the scheme.
There was a fall of over 300 ft. in the length of the site, which was about 1 Km. Escalators would facilitate transfer from different levels. The faculty buildings were generally single or double storey.

SKI RESORT IN THE VALLÉE DES BELLEVILLE, SAVOY. *Archs:* Candilis, Josic, Perriand, Piot, Prouvé, Suzuki, Woods.
This scheme was submitted in an open two stage competition. It was rejected at the outset 'being too far ahead of its time'.
Development was required for the eventual accommodation of 22,000 tourists. The nearest rail connection is at Moutiers, about 15 miles away. The road is liable to avalanches and presents continual problems of snow clearance, both on the road itself and the 70 acres parking which would be required for an estimated 7,000 cars. It was decided to eliminate the motor car. The problem became one of mechanical transportation from Moutiers to the ski station.
This was to be solved by building a monorail from Moutiers which would require a journey of only 20 minutes. At any stage this monorail could be extended to the Italian frontier post at Modane. Vertical circulation would be by escalator, ski lifts would provide facilities on the slopes. Provision was made for a helicopter landing platform.

seaside resort

7

3

4

3

2

4

3

2

4

4

3

3

2

3

2

4

Irun, France

La Coruna
Portugal

5

4

6

7

Bilbao

Photo: Karquel

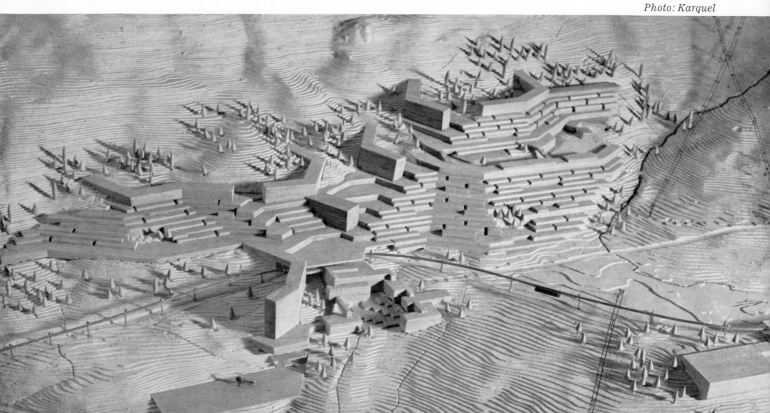

FRANKFURT: THE PROBLEMS OF A CITY
IN THE TWENTIETH CENTURY

The city is the expression of human associations and activities. Production, distribution, services and leisure each form a part of this expression. For the city, which is the home of man in society, to encourage these activities they must first be known (analysed) and then integrated (synthesized).

The city cannot result from a zoning plan; to dissociate the functions is to ignore their inter-dependence. Neither can the city be made from a composition of solids and spaces; the most perfect realization of this kind is, by definition, the most static and therefore the least adapted to the change and growth of life the town must express. Everything that happens in the city is inter-related, one event affects another.

The problem of constructing or reconstructing cities is to discover these relationships and to establish a system which creates a harmonious, complete, living organization.

This organization cannot stop at the mere harmonizing of present functions and their inter-relationships. It must also account for the evolution of change and growth. It should organize the present and lead to the future.

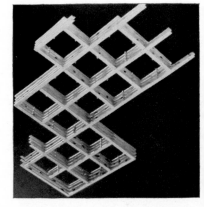

FRANKFURT. *Archs:* Candilis, Josic and Woods.
Diagrammatic model of service and pedestrian grid viewed from underneath

The problem of reconstructing the centre of Frankfurt was not to make a museum, but to discover a system which would allow the inhabitants to create their own environment with the maximum facilities, and at the same time enable it to evolve in proportion to their needs. The system proposed allows the inhabitants to control and contribute to their environment.

On the site to be rebuilt, with its existing historic monuments, it was felt that any multiplicity of individual forms would only devalue the existing buildings. But such a diversity of activities had to be included that to accommodate them in separate units would have been chaotic. To overcome this it was decided to combine all the elements in one unit keeping a valid scale both for the site and for the people using it.

The proposal is for a multi-level system composed of ducts for services related to a system of horizontal and vertical circulation for pedestrians. This system serves as a basic grid determining the areas which could be built up on a secondary structural grid inserted into the main grid. The service and supply area is contained in the basement which, on account of the sloping site, is accessible to vehicles. Under the service basement is a car park which also has easy access. Pedestrians would change levels by escalators and moving ramps.

The site of the grid was determined by the maximum span permissible without expansion joints and a span which would give economic manageable areas. These distances varied between 25 and 45 metres. The final dimension was set at 36·47 metres. The pedestrian ways are 3·66 metres wide which left a grid of free spaces for development each 32·81 metres square.

These dimensions are not arbitrary but are based on the harmonic relationship between man and space determined by Le Corbusier's Modulor. The subdivision of the areas and volumes would therefore always be related to the human scale.

Shadrach Woods

FRANKFURT. *Archs:* Candilis, Josic and Woods.
Competition entry for new centre: aerial view of model from the south with river in foreground. The m grid is visible while the building are built on the subsidiary structural grid.

Photo: Karquel

The contributions of Jean Prouvé to French building — not to say architecture — reside principally not in his invention of forms but in the clarity and simplicity of his assembly of materials. If the history of man, read in his buildings, is a record of the long evolution from mason to mechanic, Prouvé takes his place in this evolution naturally as the poet-craftsman of machined products assembly. The importance of his buildings is in their archetypal demonstrative character. He is showing us how to do it, and how worthwhile it can be to do it.

In his recent buildings, he seems at last to arrive at an architecture by the synthesis of structural clarity, function and elegance. The structure is no longer allowed to dominate as in the school at Villejuif or the Vittel pavilion. It has a part in the building but may easily be confused with the skin, or, just as easily, be allowed to stand on its own. Sometimes in the smaller buildings both conditions are present.

Prouvé's analysis of the outer skin of the building has the same clarity as Le Corbusier's. Light, ventilation, view, insulation — all these are considered, weighed and respected and developed into a special system, for each building. The functions of the membrane are first made clear and then clearly realized. This clarity (and elegance), if it goes no further, could remain cold and lifeless. But Prouvé has his own magic and makes poetry out of elegance. He restores one's faith in the machine and the mechanic. He does this by keeping control of his machine, not submitting to it but extracting from it its greatest possibilities.

The importance of the work Prouvé is doing in the present French situation cannot be overestimated. He may well be the only French builder or architect who is making a determined and successful effort to live in his own time.

Shadrach Woods

JEAN PROUVÉ
THREE
RECENT WORKS

[1]Architect? Engineer? Why bring up this question? Isn't our job simply to build?

An abundance of different things are being 'constructed' nowadays: aeroplanes, cars, machines of all kinds, machine-tools. Also housing, both private and public, is something that is 'constructed' like the things above-mentioned. In the case of the former, however, the question is never raised as to how the job was divided up among different people in an industrial setting where the work is done in accordance with the prevailing spirit of teamwork.

Every single object that is to be created grows out of a 'constructive idea'. Man in his capacity as creator sees it spontaneously as a ready-made object; the materials that he is thoroughly familiar with have inspired him and led him to his creative decision.

Then comes the problem of execution. All the technicians required combine in a team and process the 'idea', which they are obliged to respect. Only, they are permitted, in cases where the idea is technically intractable, to modify it slightly from the original creative intention. This frequently leads to the overthrow of the original idea, which means that the idea was not worth very much to begin with. A beautiful aeroplane, a bridge with the same qualities, cannot be built with this team of people standing behind the 'idea'.

Aeroplane constructors and builders of dams do not style themselves architects? And an architect is also compelled to become an engineer; if he is not one, he is not in a position really to defend his creative conception.

The architect, like the creator of industrial products, is dependent on a team of engineers without whose specialized knowledge he cannot build.

There are men who were trained as engineers and are no doubt great architects. The reverse is also true. However, we know that many architects are nothing but construction stylists. This is what occurs to one when one gets into a discussion of the status of the architect and the engineer. And that is bad indeed!

Ordinarily the architect along with his assistants has an office. He or the engineers who advise him also have their office and associates. The given construction firm, for its part, has its special associates, engineers, foremen and workmen; thus there are three autonomous organizations all jealously bent on furthering their own privileges. The men on the job can do nothing but vent their criticism of a thing which they themselves have not designed and, finally, they go ahead and carry out — at least in part — their own ideas. If then the architect weakens or if his conception is a bad one, everything is watered down. And that's what we call compromise!

In my opinion, the desirable break-down of functions would be as follows:

Architect/Engineer/Designer/Contractor

There are, I repeat, various functional organs. Every single object except the building construction job is handled by one single organization, by one single industry, by one single contractor. Once you get a clear picture of the evil besetting us, you will realize that the building is the only thing that is created by a freely working professional man. This is the reason why architecture is lagging behind! This is the reason why—in contrast to the relentless progress in industry—progress in the building trade is so insignificant!

Jean Prouvé

Entrance porch. Large panels are faced with plywood and smaller panels are of adjustable glass louvres.

[1] Reproduced with kind permission from Bauen + Wohnen.

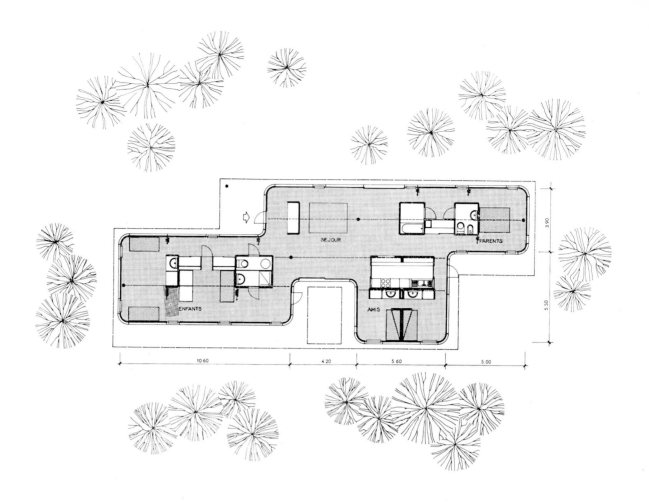

HOUSE AT BEAUVALLON

Architect/Engineer

Jean Prouvé

Photo: Pierre Joly—Vera Cardot

Detail of glass louvred ventilator unit and mullions

Detail of entrance porch. Note quarter round ply corner unit

Photos: Pierre Joly—Vera Cardot

General interior view showing storage unit
forming portion of kitchen with R.S.J. over

Interior view of storage unit showing supporting R.S.J. over

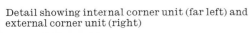

Detail showing internal corner unit (far left) and
external corner unit (right)

Internal view of bedroom showing corner. Note light and switches
on back plate of mullion which contains electrical cables

Detail of corner showing quarter-round panel and mullions

HOUSE AT ST DIÉ

Architect/Engineer

Jean Prouvé

Photos: Pierre Joly—Vera Cardot

Interior showing exposed steelwork, sliding aluminium window and the pre-formed timber panels of the ceiling which are carried through to form the external soffit and abut against a pressed aluminium gutter. The house is built out over a sloping site on a masonry base which contains a cellar.

Detail of entrance door inserted into reeded aluminium panel

Detail of sliding window   Interior

OFFICE AT AUBERVILLIERS

Architect/Engineer

Jean Prouvé

Photos: Pierre Joly—Vera Cardot

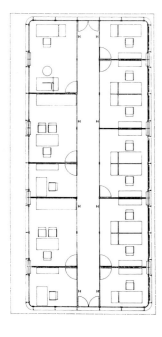

Exterior. Two sizes of units are used. The larger type are fixed windows, the lower section being obscure glass, while the upper portion is clear. The horizontal joint between the two sheets is secured by a Neoprene strip which is visible in the photograph. The smaller unit is an adjustable louvred panel which also has a vertical mullion to take interval partitions and allows, when necessary, two offices to be ventilated from one unit.

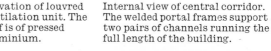

PLAN. The roof projects further on the south side to provide shade from the sun.

Elevation of louvred ventilation unit. The roof is of pressed aluminium.

Internal view of central corridor. The welded portal frames support two pairs of channels running the full length of the building.

SWITZERLAND

Contributing Editor

Bernhard Hoesli

House at Olten 1958 *Photo: Albert Winkler*

Boiler factory at Thun 1959 *Photo: Albert Winkler*

House at Motier 1959 *Photo: Albert Winkler*

House at Flamatt 1960 *Photo: Leonardo Bezzola*

Siedlung Halen
and the Eclectic Predicament

Halen erupts from a hillside a few miles outside Bern like a cellular geological phenomenon. It is intriguing by its paradoxical openness and fortress-like introversion. The irregularity of its brise-soleil gives it an alert aspect, and its quality of delight and pleasure compels an almost instant childlike approval before a more rational and critical process can intervene to test its validity.

Halen, like all the work of Atelier 5, is Corbusian in detail, and the plan is just one step away from that of the Permanent City of the St Baume project. It must be seen as one scheme of many expressing the Atelier 5 attitude towards a current architectural predicament, the problem of progress towards a general architecture.

In the non-style intentions of International Architecture lay confidence in the growth of a twentieth-century vernacular, based on a faith in rationalism, a misconception of the role of technology and a rather simple-minded psychology. Its achievements were impressive. At best, its forms were modest, aims objective, and the problem itself took priority over any subjective, expressionist intentions of the architect. However, the movement was never general enough nor broadly enough based to satisfy a subsequent generation of architects. The predicament remains. In fact, as each year passes, the need for a disinterested approach becomes more pressing. For the work of many talented architects is seen to be more frequently an indulgence in individual virtuosity, rather than an attempt to correlate the problem at hand with the problem at large.

In this situation, the eclecticism of Atelier 5, or any other group with a similar attitude, is something of an act of faith. It affirms that if the future course is not clear, to progress at all it is necessary to adopt the successful forms and idioms of the immediate past and thus avoid working endlessly over the same ground or degenerating into a chaotic individualism. It is therefore wise to choose the best source, use it without rigidity, and progress from there. It contains a plea to all architects to climb on to the same wagon.

However, such an attitude forces the architect into a position which repudiates the basis of his decision. It is bound to be sectarian and, by avoiding the need to redefine the nature of the whole problem at its most general in each programme, misses the very level from which a contribution to a general approach can be valid. For a common architectural language is valid only by common consent, and the effort to arrive at this point involves a constant search for the fundamental interrelations of the whole of society, and the expression of the appropriate generality in each programme. To choose an eclectic position in a culture as disoriented as ours seems to edge the architect into unique essays in style that are finally as abortive as the work of the most self-indulgent designer.

If this point of view is correct, one is entitled to look with a certain suspicion both at schemes which are too unique and exhibitionistic and those whose vocabulary is too blatantly eclectic, for both imply that a responsibility has been abandoned. Halen, for all its achievements, is vulnerable to this charge.

It is fair to take for comparison the Neubühl Cité d'Habitation, a typical example of international architecture. In this scheme no need was felt to exploit or distort elements expressively beyond their sheer functional role, and what was rationally subsidiary was kept subsidiary. The designers' intentions were to deal with all things with a maximum modesty and intrude with their fantasies to a minimum. It is quite simply a well-arranged middle-class housing estate built to what was then a relatively high suburban density of about 80 to the acre, providing its own local amenities. Isolated by virtue of its situation on an open wooded site, Neubühl would remain unaffected by intrusions of subsequent buildings or by the spread of Zürich, as it is absolutely direct.

Halen, unlike Neubühl, cannot be considered as a prototype, but is unique. It is carefully contrived as one complete object that not only does not permit growth and change, but assumes in its design that conditions around it will be unchanging. Its atmosphere is vulnerable, and it depends for its success on the unique character of the site.

In detail, basically irrational and emotional intentions are conveyed by a clever distortion of Corbusian forms.

Corbusier has in fact used brise-soleils expressively, but always in a manner which establishes a proper relationship both to the block as a whole and to the individual units behind. At Halen we find almost exactly the same elements. But, by an inversion, the brise-soleils are the most prominent features on the site, exceeding the houses in height and massiveness. The whole cellular complex of plinths, garden walls and roofs, brise-soleils and terracing of the site seem to belong to the order of the rock beneath, and play a dominant role, against and into which the relatively insubstantial houses nestle. The walls of the houses externally are white, and become slight and papery by comparison with the rough concrete elements. To engage the forms, a slight confusion is indulged in with the concrete externally, as it does not exactly conform to the limits of the internal space of the houses behind. The precast coping at the eaves is, oddly, neither engaged with the brise-soleil nor separate and part of the house, yet it has the effect of continuing the primary order of rock over the house itself and capping it. These mannerist expedients serve to delineate a progression throughout, which is only completed in the living-rooms themselves. For if Halen is conceived as a piece of central Bern which has in a sense broken off and floated away in a sea of trees, within itself it presents a series of progressive centricities. Its total form reads with the cabalistic unity of a mannerist town. Nothing is residual, and its components constitute the boundaries to its own centre, the little piazza.

To emphasize the progression of scale, the interior of the houses, in contrast to the texture of the whole, is spare and economical, minimum in feeling, compared with the lavishness of spirit that has been indulged in fashioning the external elements. The houses are entirely private, the only infringement being from the living-room balcony, from which it is possible to overlook your neighbour's garden.

All the public space in Halen is paved and bounded by walls. The houses, however, have small courtyards in front and gardens behind (if you can speak of front and back) in which plants grow with tropical profusion and the atmosphere is enchanting. Nevertheless, Halen can be seen as an exercise in style, establishing a certain dependency on its adjacent city and emphasizing levels of privacy within itself. It is interesting that neither issue seems to have concerned the designers of Neubühl. Personally, I regret that the architects felt it necessary to clothe the design in so elaborate an architectural dress. All their intentions could have been more aptly and directly satisfied, with a gain in freshness and simplicity, by a less contorted expression. My feeling is that the eclectic position they have assumed involves them in these techniques. I do not want to minimize the achievement of Halen, or to suggest that it does not create a delightful livable environment. It plays its game with skill and poise. However, since buildings do not live by virtue only of their plastic success, but also by the relationships they imply, the danger of exploiting a particular project on the level of its uniqueness is that a false or fantasy position may be assumed *à propos* the society or culture within which the building exists. It is fair to wonder if so introverted and protected an atmosphere is really required, or whether its charm will last. Perhaps this also is the result of adopting a Corbusian plan and therefore cutting short the creative process itself.[1]

Neave Brown

[1] Reproduced by kind permission of *Architectural Design*

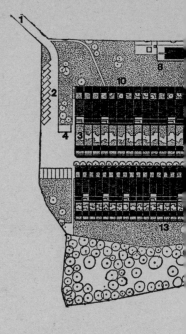

SIEDLUNG HALEN SITE PLAN

KEY

1 Approach road
2 Car park
3 Central garage
4 Petrol station
5 Village square
6 Shops and café

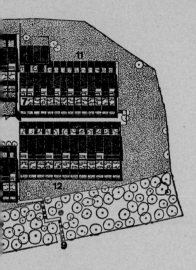

7 Centre for heating, electricity,
   water, and laundries
8 Swimming pool and playground
9 Pedestrian access
10 Upper row of houses, type 12
11 Upper row of houses, type 380
12 Lower row of houses, type 12
13 Lower row of houses, type 380
14 Studios

A Reply from the Architects

We have been invited to reply to Neave Brown's article. We cannot do more than touch on his arguments because his way of 'experiencing' architecture is alien to us. We will therefore limit ourselves to explaining under what conditions he 'experienced' Halen and how his experience stands in relation to our own views on the subject. Finally, we shall reply to a few of his detailed points.

Mr Brown surveys the evolution of twentieth century architecture. It is a matter of considerable concern to him that it is developing in a healthy and purposeful manner. He has drawn up for himself a kind of order of this evolution. Armed with these preconceptions, he looks at our Estate and reacts only to those elements that fit into or conflict with his pre-established notions. The reader will have already noticed that he reacts primarily to the visually emphasized parts of the building. He notes these down as characteristic and compares them with the pre-established order of his own. This way of experiencing things is familiar to us; it is common to us all. But, as we consider a question at greater length, our thoughts become adjusted, the centres of gravity shift and our assessments change. Mr Brown was unable to give the Halen question sufficient attention to reach this second stage. He reacted as described mainly on the visually emphasized building features such as loggias, brise-soleils and roof tops. These elements have largely determined his classification of our contribution to twentieth-century architecture.

As we have already stated, it is not our intention to criticize how he interprets our contribution; we shall merely indicate the difference between his point of view and our own. The above building elements assume an exaggerated importance for Mr Brown insomuch as they fit in with his way of thinking. But in point of fact, they are the result of *our* thought. To put it into the simplest terms; in the planning of Halen, we subordinated the exterior expression of function to our experience of the interior space and to the most economic method of construction. Now, it is unfortunately the case in building that a correctly and economically constructed building element does not contain of itself the visual form which corresponds to its significance. It is not, therefore, the case, as Mr Brown would have it, that we have 'distorted' the forms to give them the required weight, but that we ought to have 'distorted' them until they had assumed *less* importance.

The direction our thought has taken can be partially ascribed to the view-point of a Halen resident. As can be seen from the physical situation, the façades play only a minor role; they are almost hidden from view. It is left to the interested viewer to climb over the garden wall to study the main frontages so that he can pass judgement on the architects. This we had not envisaged.

How far Mr Brown's opinions are the result of his pre-occupation with the surface aspect is revealed by the comparison he draws with the Neubühl Housing of 1930. The plain expression of the houses in Neubühl is not so much a question of style as the expression of a substantially simpler functionalism. Neubühl is one of the familiar terrace form estates of the period executed by good architects. The essential difference lies in the simple function, not the simple form.

The obtrusiveness of the exterior elements of Halen is not merely a matter of style but arises above all from the compact way of building which demands that the building be conceived as a complete entity. The majority of onlookers are making their first acquaintance with this phenomenon in more recent architecture and are unable to escape from this impression of obtrusiveness. But in compacted building, it is indispensable to conceive the thing as a whole and thereby create the necessary atmosphere.

Possibility of Expansion: It is impossible to enlarge Halen; in accordance with our forest regulations, the protective forest belt is inviolate. Take heed! We had no intention of putting forward an example that should be a general prototype. Halen, as it stands, should not be imitated on any other site nor be considered as a blueprint for future towns.

Social Mixing: We did not lose sight of the question of scale. Halen has 280 residents and is not a 'district'. The fact that it is limited to people in a certain income group is tied up with the problem of discovering a formula for family unit building. A mixture of different social groups on this scale would, in our view, be inadvisable.

Eclecticism: It is not easy to produce something authentically new. We ask for a little time. It is true that we have taken over some elements from Le Corbusier and that the exterior appearance of our houses can give rise to reflections as expressed by Mr Brown. However, we beg the reader to judge from the illustrations that follow what importance should be accorded to what aspects.

Atelier 5

SIEDLUNG HALEN HOUSING, BERN

Architects

Atelier 5   Fritz, Gerber, Herterberg, Hostettler, Morgenthaler, Pini and Thornann

The Aim: The desire for undisturbed privacy in a healthy community is a wholly justifiable one and capable of fulfilment even today. It is, however, self-evident that it is no longer possible to build each family unit on the lines of the superior middle-class house, that is as a villa standing on a half or three-quarter acre plot. For good or ill one has to be content with a smaller building area from one seventh to one fifth of an acre — according to the individual purse — on which to build the dream house in question — a miniature country house or middle-class residence — full of references to a past context. The superior middle-class house is degraded to a four and a half roomed house, the stately farm house to a small garage. And all too soon the attractive view (insofar as it existed) is obstructed by an inconsiderate neighbour, no less eager to realize *his* dream house. What results is a dreary estate of family unit houses with a number of small streets which it is impossible to keep free of petrol fumes and where children cannot play without danger from traffic. Any hope of undisturbed privacy is ruled out. The Halen scheme was an attempt to achieve a fundamentally new concept. In order to attain this object at a reasonable figure, ways and means had to be found within the legal terms of reference for setting the density substantially above that which is the normal practice on the family unit house estate.

The Concept: Individual ownership of one's house and joint ownership of all the communal facilities as items of equal importance.

Thus every dwelling-unit carries with it four and a half acres of available space with streets, paths, greenswards and woodland. The communal facilities on the estate include central-heating plant and hot-water services; laundrettes; the large swimming-pool, sports field and playground; garage for all the cars and petrol and car-service station. A caretaker's house also forms part of the communal property. The caretaker is an employee of the property company and is responsible for the running and maintenance of all the communal facilities.

The Halen Estate stands on land belonging to the Commune of Kirchlindach on the left above the Halen Bridge over the Wohlensee. It is only three miles from the centre of the nearby city, but the region has retained its rural character right up to the present time.

A forest clearing of some six acres with a pronounced slope towards the south and an impressive long-distance view over the Bremgartenwald as far as the Alps was available for the realization of the proposed scheme.

Two standard-type houses, with four variations (four to six rooms with and without sun-parlour), together with some studios, small dwelling houses, shop and restaurant and all the pertaining communal amenities formed the layout programme.

Photo: Albert Winkler

Photo: Albert Winkler

View along central axis from the
east

Covered way to central piazza, shop
and restaurant

Stepped ramp to houses above piazza

Brise-soleils, balconies and gardens

Photos: Albert Winkler

Pedestrian Access

Photos: Albert Winkler

Communal Facilities

Photo: Christian Moser

Right: Studio flats on pedestrian way to piazza

Interiors

Photos: Albert Winkler

Gardens

Photos: Albert Winkler

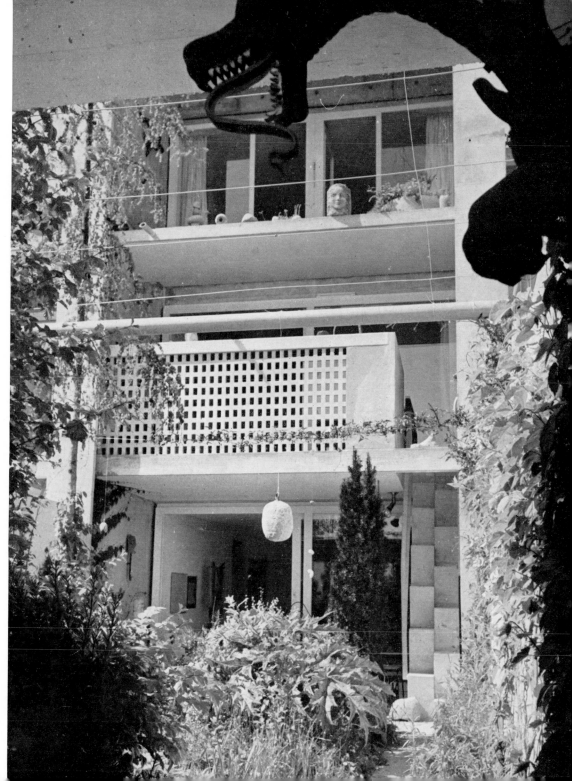

SECONDARY SCHOOL, AESCH

Architects

Forderer, Otto and Zwimpfer

This scheme won an open competition in 1958. It provides nine classrooms each for thirty-six children, eleven specialized classrooms, a large assembly hall, gymnasium and playroom. The school buildings are concentrated in the centre of a level site standing clear of the low-level residential suburb that surrounds it. In style and character it aggressively and intentionally dominates the non-architecture of the suburb. The ubiquitous rough-shuttered concrete has been moulded into a tough monolith, the raw surface continuing into the courts and gardens in geometrical play sculptures, walls, steps and pyramids. The total effect is starkly consistent, as uncompromising in the triple-height circulation gallery of the main building interior as in the deeply etched bands of windows outside.

The main three-storey teaching building is flanked on either side by the lower gymnasium and assembly hall blocks, with open spaces and playgrounds integrated between the buildings, and is tightly defined by a concrete parapet retaining wall, pierced, slotted and shaped with the same architectonic mannerisms that characterize the detailing throughout. Circulation through and between the buildings is open and informal. There is plenty of space. The consistently chunky treatment of all surfaces creates a close relationship between inside and outside and goes a long way towards establishing a continuous flow of space that dissolves the rigid separation of interior and exterior.

The whole building shouts with a coarse voice, every skilfully contrived detail clamouring for attention. The visual noise cannot quite conceal the self-consciousness of the language.

Photos: F. Maurer *Below* Main approach *Right* Sculptured space between blocks

Photos: F. Maurer

Upper floor gallery access to
classrooms

Triple height main entrance hall
with interlocking staircases

Photos: F. Maurer

Assembly hall

GERMANY

Contributing Editor

Erhard Duwenhogger

WOLFSBURG CULTURAL CENTRE

Architect

Alvar Aalto

Photo: Heidersberger

Ground floor ambulatory and shops. Marble-faced upper storey rests on copper-clad columns

The humming production lines of the Volkswagen have transformed a rural medieval village into a twentieth-century town which symbolizes *par excellence* the material prosperity of a society based on the interdependence of man and machine. In twenty-five years a compact urban unit has grown up, free from intermediate provincial stages, developing as rapidly and vigorously as its pulsing industrial heart demands.

This lively young town, with its living areas clearly defined in the hilly landscape, surrounds a growing administrative centre in which the municipality reserved land for a building to be devoted to the cultural life of the town. It was to be an antidote to the negative aspects of material prosperity — the soul-destroying monotony of factory work, the isolation of family life in lifeless residential suburbs — an attempt to create in the heart of the city a centre for recreation, education and creative activity; to replace suburban existence with urban life.

Aalto's plan won a limited competition because he combined the three major parts of the programme in one building and established the closest possible connection between the variety of functions the centre was to house: libraries, adult education centre, youth recreation centre and shopping, together with all the administrative and office accommodation they will require.

The heart of the building is strictly arranged in a tight rectilinear form, but develops characteristically in plan and section with increasing freedom. In the plan this culminates in the free form of the five auditoria whose irregular polygonal façades dominate the exterior composition. The section grows from an entrance lobby overlooking the City Hall square, and, as with the plan, becomes increasingly free, allowing Aalto to introduce characteristic subtleties of top lighting to the libraries and auditoria and creating a variety of spaces that flow naturally and inevitably together in a finely controlled sequence.

Aalto has designed all the furniture and light fittings for the building. The materials he uses inside and out — marble, copper, wood and ceramics — are all brought together with a patient attention to detail, although one might question the need to bring marbles from Italy, Greece and Sweden to make a woven façade treatment that seems curiously unrelated to the plan, structure or needs of the building.

Many of the external details derive directly from Aalto's well-known structures in brick and timber. It is odd and rather disquieting to see them imitated in marble, and paradoxical that he should combine such durable materials with an internal finish of white-painted plaster that can hardly survive rigorous use for long. The cultural centre may become bruised and dented, but in the process it may also establish itself as the living heart of the town.

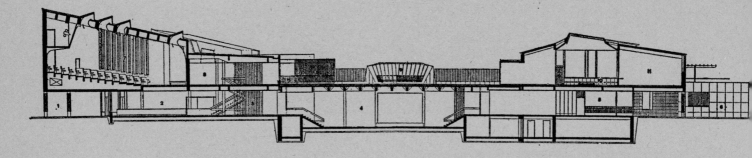

SECTION KEY

1 Covered portico
2 Entrance hall with cloakroom
3 Main stairway
4 Hall for dancing and games

5 Entrance to children's library
6 Children's yard
7 Large lecture hall
8 Upper hall

9 Roof terrace
10 Group area with open fireplace
11 Workshop for wood and metal

PLAN KEY

1 Studio
2 Lecture room
3 Lecture room
4 Lecture room
5 Lecture room

6 Lecture room
7 Wood and metal workroom
8 Ceramic workroom
9 Inner courtyard
10 Clubroom

11 Club and table tennis room
12 Caretaker's flat
13 Assistant's flat
14 Director's flat

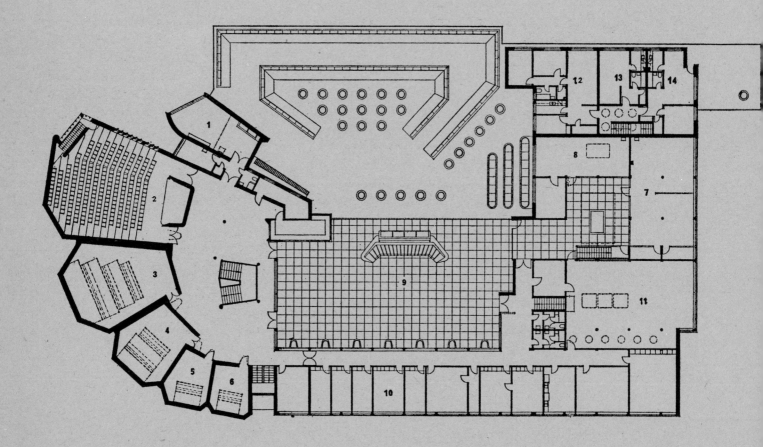

The studio and lecture rooms cluster round the roof terrace

182

An irregular profile of marble-clad
walls screens the town hall square

Photos: Heidersberger

Blind wall to the library with the
studio and large lecture hall

Detail of studio window and louvred
side-light to large lecture hall

Above Staircase to upper hall with view through to roof terrace

Right Cloakroom hall with stairs to upper level and lecture halls

Left Large lecture hall interior

Below Large library with gallery at ground floor level

Photos: *Heidersberger*

Street elevation

Right Garden elevation
Sculptor's studio and dining room

STUDIO HOUSE, HAMBURG

Architect

Timm Ohrt

The programme for this family house and sculptor's studio required rapid, inexpensive construction with provision for the studio to be self-contained so that the house could be let.

By adopting a system of pre-fabricated timber braced by screening walls of brick, the architect achieved a construction period of five months.

The site is in the middle of a small group of houses on the outskirts of Hamburg between the Elbe and a park. Because the access street is used by a large number of pedestrians, an adequate shield for the rooms overlooking the garden was essential.

The living area is planned around a double-height ceiling, with large glass sliding doors opening on to the view over the countryside and on to a private garden. A gallery creates a windowless 'hidden' sitting-room above. The studio, also double-height, contains a spiral stair leading to the living accommodation above.

188

Photos: Wolfgang Etzold

Below Ground floor living area

THYSSEN HOUSE, DÜSSELDORF

Architects

Hentrich and Petschnigg

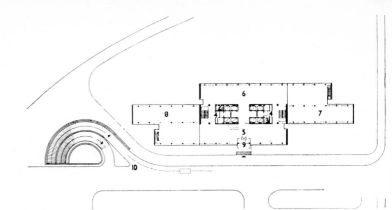

Photo: Arno Wrubel

PLAN KEY

1 Elevator lobby
2 Firemen's lift
3 Service
4 Duct
5 Entrance hall
6, 7, 8 Reception and offices
9 Lobby
10 Ramp to parking

The skyscraper forms an immense architectural limb in the centre of Düsseldorf between the crowded business centre and the peace of the Hofgarten. Its steep, windowless, narrow side dominates busy Jan-Willem-Platz on the south. The broad window frontages face west towards the old town and the Rhine, and east towards the newer parts of the town. The plan develops around a closely packed service and circulation core and is articulated to create the impression of three separate slabs, bunched close together in an attempt to reduce the massiveness of the total ensemble.

The steel skeleton structure of the skyscraper is supported on a separate foundation of reinforced concrete encased in a watertight tank that 'floats' on the high underground water level and contains mechanical services and a two-storey garage with access down a spiral ramp.

Mechanical equipment includes complete air conditioning (there are no opening windows), with short and long range lifts serving different parts of the building. High-ceilinged reception and entrance halls looking out through glazed screens to the surrounding parkland lead to the eighteen office floors which can be freely planned with interchangeable partitioning. Above these are the directors' and executives' suites with clubrooms and dining rooms on the topmost floors.

Photo: Arno Wrubel

THYSSEN HOUSE
double-height entrance hall

NETHERLANDS

Contributing Editor

Herman Hertzberger

Photo: J. Hammer

The steps — too low and too long for easy sitting — are mostly occupied by youngsters and tourists, ignorant, uninterested, in any case not at all, or hardly, impressed by the intended symbol, sometimes more or less demonstrative, reclining or even stretched out on the street opposite the royal palace in Amsterdam.

A monument to war victims becomes a place to sit; in such a way that the sitting itself becomes the true monument in spite of itself and its designers.

Photo: J. Hammer

The Permeable Surface of the City

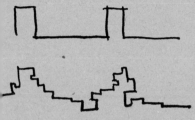

In Holland, more than anywhere else in the world, the intensive use of the available surface must always be borne in mind, for nowhere are so many people to be found together in so little space. In addition, the need for enclosure must be greater here than anywhere, since nowhere is the horizon broken by hills or woods, nor does the flat, soft ground co-operate in any way. Thus, the arguments are evident for close and intensive building in this most open land in the world. It is, therefore, the most incredible paradox that people are busy in this town, Holland, wasting space on an extensive scale. These extension schemes for the large cities — garden cities — produce neither gardens nor cities, and there is no possible link when both components are lacking. Architects are destroying places while creating a void, where there is already so much void and so little space. In blocks which are spatially set apart at such a distance that the shadow of one block does not even reach another, everyone is an outsider, lost between walls of unassailable smoothness whose impermeability can never accept, but only reject. A flat unbroken floor induces one to go on, a smooth wall can only be passed; it keeps its distance, withdraws, and offers no resistance. The first stage in the formation of enclosure is the resistance of floor and wall; it is this resistance which causes one to slow down or accelerate, which can influence the rhythm of existence: i.e., the forming of our surroundings into enclosure: town.

To make our dwellings habitable, we must create *enclosure*[1]; *enclosure* for shelter, shelter for both spirit and heart. The larger the world becomes, and the further men travel, the greater the need becomes for *enclosure*, and part of our work is to give the widest significance to these two extremes by reconciling them with one another. Our environment is created: chiselled out, coagulated, stretched, extended, like a fold in the ground, so that room is made available for everyone and everything.

'Town' is the integrity that results from the intensive contouring of the surface: it is the total *enclosure*, brought about in such a way that the largest possible number of people can be absorbed. Usually, the first lead is given by the contours of the ground itself. Even the most insignificant change — difference in level, incline, hollow (everywhere that dust is arrested in its flow and piles up) — is formative of *enclosure* and can be the prelude to town.

In the design of the Lijnbaan, as well as in the playgrounds, we are concerned with a conception extending over a long period of time. In neither case is consideration of the whole possible, and we can only judge them in the framework of their process of development. Growth and change are the only constant factors in the image of the town, while every stage of continuous rebuilding must be permanent. Therefore every new encroachment must be a complete contribution in itself; a fulfilling of the time, an articulation of the surface.

Here 'articulation' means a disintegration of this surface in such a way as to give it size, enabling it to envelop everything that takes place within. Through this development, walls no longer function as partitions but as bases; the wall as 'enclosure'. As such a process of articulation advances, a town becomes more concentrated, deeper in outline and of increasing capacity. Little room in much space becomes much room.

Our starting point in planning must be the provision of optimum capacity. Clearly, thinking in 'functions' — the fruit of 19th-century causality — is inadequate for this purpose. The functional city does not keep up with the times; when its plans are ready to leave the drawing-board they are already out of date.

In the generative process of the town the ingredients continually change their meaning, i.e., the meaning migrates. Therefore, it is impossible to say that every part has its specific place in the whole; the shifting of the significance also changes the balance of strength between relationships. (In the 17th century the Amsterdam canals were the most important highways for commercial purposes of those days; they fulfilled the function for which they were intended. Now their significance is changed into a tourist attraction. Is it, then, pure chance that in present-day circumstances and with their new significance, they are still not badly situated?)

Every form must be polyvalent and capable of withstanding such changes in significance, in order to remain meaningful in a situation which is always renewing itself. In giving form to this metamorphosis we cannot start from preconceived notions. Naturally, we can make our intentions clear to the person concerned by drawing up a programme (in our attempt to give him what we think he desires). But will he fall into the trap of our set programme?

The form we decide upon must be voluntarily directed towards a certain purpose, and, thanks to the secret intentions of the designer, must be suggestive as regards every other possible content. It is the rhythm of existence that decides the meaning of things, and thus form and content provoke one another.

House is there, where one feels at home (everywhere should be home); a town without playgrounds (since all is playground).

(1) The Dutch word *interieur* has no exact English equivalent and has been translated throughout the text as *enclosure* to express a *quality* of space. *Enclosure* in the sense used here has philosophical connotations implying identity and significance — the difference between *somewhere* and *anywhere* — and the creation of a sense of *place*. (Editor)

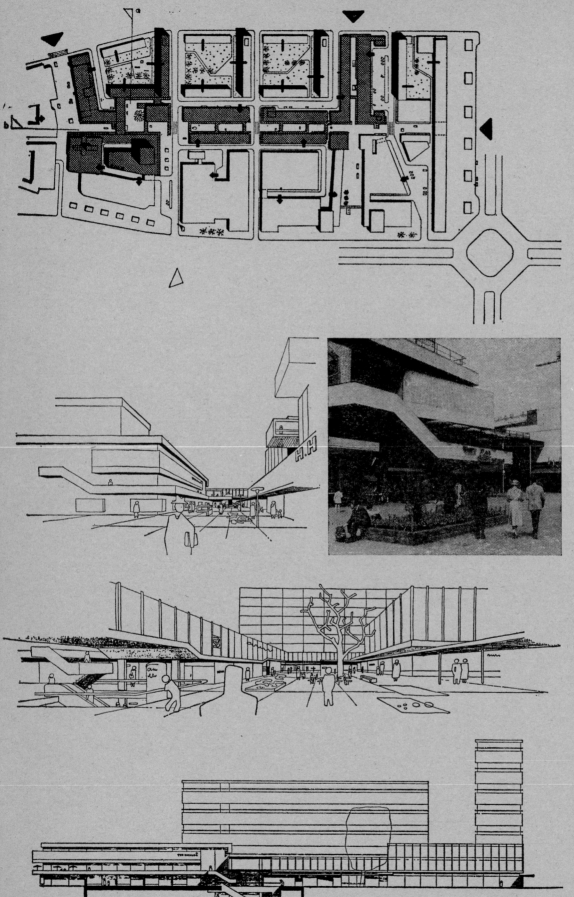

The last proposed extension to the Lijnbaan in Rotterdam, designed by Van den Broek and Bakema, forms the completion of this shopping centre, of which the greater part dates from 1953. This last link connects the existing part with the two blocks of shops built in 1951 and 1953 by the same architects.

Between these two existing parts an enclosed square is planned, which will be surrounded by high buildings.

An art centre will be situated on this square, as a bridge across the longitudinal axis of the Lijnbaan street, with an excavation under the passage leading to a News Cinema and a Jazz Cellar.

The whole complex (strictly for pedestrians only), can achieve very intense dynamism through its many covered passages and highly mobile rows of shops with window displays and furnishings. The excavation will be the culminating point of the whole complex.

Clearly, it is only right that, thanks to the complexity of the design, such compactness has been achieved within the framework of such a limited area, that once again a comparison with the centres of old towns comes to mind. Although it is still far from being Verona, this centre does not fall far short of achieving the density which we need quite as much as do the Southern lands, albeit for completely opposite motives.

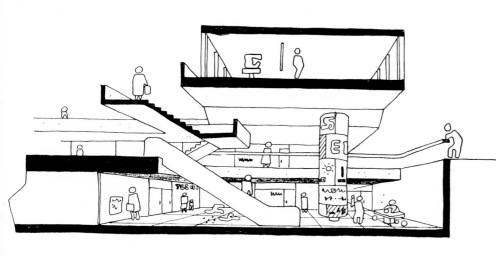

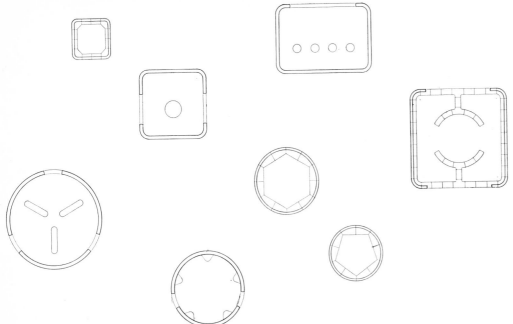

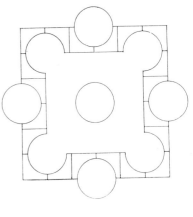

Close to the ground are the children; they find their way into all the open pores of the streets, walls and roofs.

In the old town there is still the adventure of doorsteps and holes and corners, and a lot of other dangerous companions, like traffic and water.

There is absolutely no provision at all for the smallest children. The Public Works Service in Amsterdam commissioned Aldo van Eyck to design an extensive programme of playgrounds.

In the course of about 15 years, more than 400 have been completed, at first on empty lots. In the new districts they are situated in open spaces, lost among the housing blocks.

These playgrounds consist of a collection of a number of certain basic elements, in each case put together in different combinations, depending on situation, space and possibilities. One story; always different, with endless variations on the same theme.

Photo: Dienst

Photo: Dienst

Photo: Dienst

Photo: Dienst

There are enclosed domes, vaults and other aluminium structures, variously interpreted as trees, hills or tent-house-frame. Further there are discs, potential islands and tables, and sand-pits in a great variety of forms. These elements are able to colour the surroundings in which they are placed, while themselves taking on the colour of the surroundings, although always managing to retain their own character; thus they follow the correct middle path between being too much themselves (expression) and too little themselves (neutrality); balancing on the razor-edge between fit for nothing and unfit for everything; the only way that can lead to anything further. At the most unexpected points in the most uninteresting districts one can come across spots that give one suddenly a feeling of town; an insertion of small pieces of new tissue that give a clear insight into what the town might have been.

Photo: Louis van Paridon

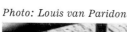

Photo: Dienst

199

Photo: Violette Cornelius

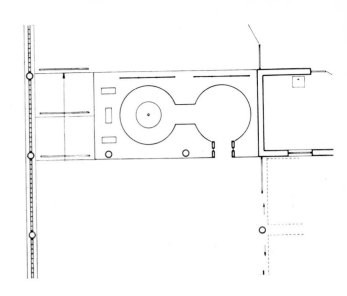

Photo: Aldo van Eyck

The playgrounds of Van Eyck are
for the children — the difference
between adults and children is too
naïve here — substitutes, where
town has been amputated, and cannot fulfil itself any more.
In his Children's Home we find the
same kind of elements, though
here not artificially introduced,
but of its very substance; the
permeable surface of the city,
providing places for every
fulfilment.

Photo: Louis van Paridon

Photo: Louis van Paridon

Photo: Louis van Paridon

FINLAND

Contributing Editor

Esko Lehesmaa

Reima Pietila

Architecture is usually presented in a standardized form: contrived photographs (super-tidy rooms with ashtrays, art magazines and a woman's profile mathematically arranged), standard drawings (for the benefit of the block-makers), and a short explanation by the architect, adding up the square feet, telling you the centres of the columns, giving a brief résumé about the site and its climate and ending up with a list of electrical engineers and contractors. Rarely does a book or magazine transmit an *impression* of the nature of architectural creation, the processes that contribute to its final form. Man is born in architecture, he lives and dies in architecture — must he be buried in the floor plan?

The appreciation of architecture should be retrospective, connecting the first tentative thoughts with the finished building, to reflect the same time-sequence that accompanied the creation: from idea to reality. This is usually impossible. By the time the building is finished all sketches, preliminary layouts and tentative ideas have disappeared. The frozen photographs capture only one arbitrary moment in the long process. The subjective vision of the photographer can be seriously misleading. Compare any building with its photographs.

Reima Pietila has designed two of the most remarkable recent projects in Finland; both are the result of competitions and will be constructed this year. The Kaleva Church is in Tampere, the second largest industrial city after Helsinki, often called the Manchester of Finland. The Dipoli (a clubhouse for the Student Corps of the Helsinki Institute of Technology) will be at Otaniemi, six miles from Helsinki.

A sense of humour is rarely accepted in the visual arts, never in architecture; in student club houses in Scandinavia it has long been a tradition to design with levity, a tongue-in-cheek architecture if you like. (Pietila labelled his competition entry 'Wedding March of the Cave Men'.) In these two projects he manipulates light, form, structure and materials to create two diametrically opposite atmospheres: a vivacious and boisterous students' club and the sacred stillness of a church.

203

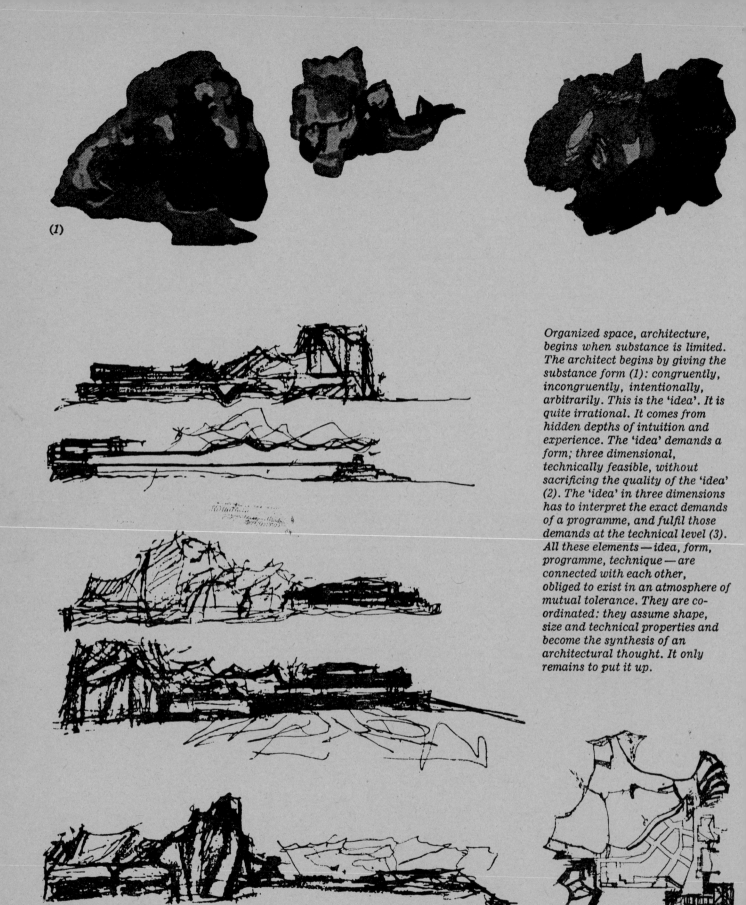

(1)

Organized space, architecture, begins when substance is limited. The architect begins by giving the substance form (1): congruently, incongruently, intentionally, arbitrarily. This is the 'idea'. It is quite irrational. It comes from hidden depths of intuition and experience. The 'idea' demands a form; three dimensional, technically feasible, without sacrificing the quality of the 'idea' (2). The 'idea' in three dimensions has to interpret the exact demands of a programme, and fulfil those demands at the technical level (3). All these elements — idea, form, programme, technique — are connected with each other, obliged to exist in an atmosphere of mutual tolerance. They are co-ordinated: they assume shape, size and technical properties and become the synthesis of an architectural thought. It only remains to put it up.

(2)

(3)

STUDENTS UNION, OTANIEMI

Architect

Reima Pietila

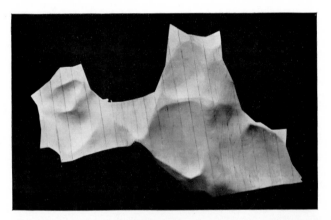

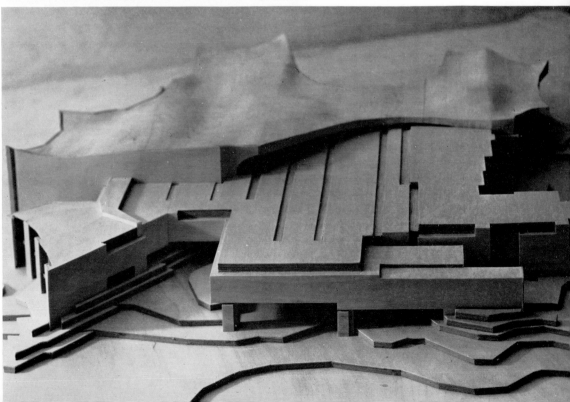

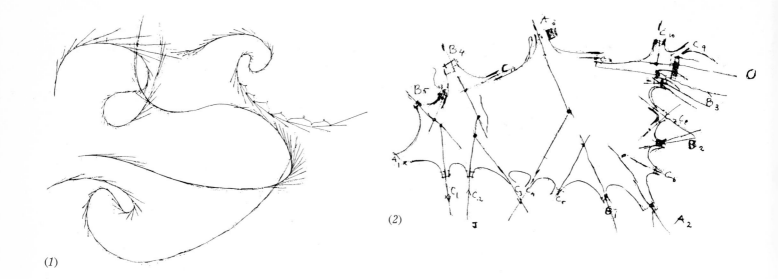

(1)

(2)

KALEVA CHURCH, TAMPERE

Architect

Reima Pietila

Space exists through form, form exists through light, touch and sound. Architecture begins with the organization of light. A sacred space is the purest form of architectural experience. Its function is to communicate transcendental reality. Direct light and reflected light are studied; the amount, direction, intensity and quality of the light are determined (1). The three-dimensional effect of sunlight limits, determines and controls the basic plan form (2). Light enters the space through transparent wall elements, and its quality is transformed into the substance of the interior (3). The quality of surfaces depends on their material: cold, warm, rough, smooth, hard or soft. The materials are analysed (4). The space (sacred space) exists through light.

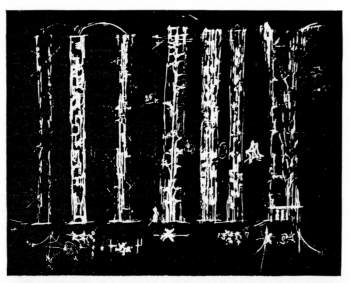

(3)

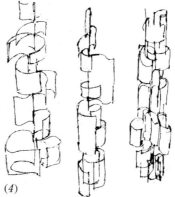

(4)

Photos: Pietinen

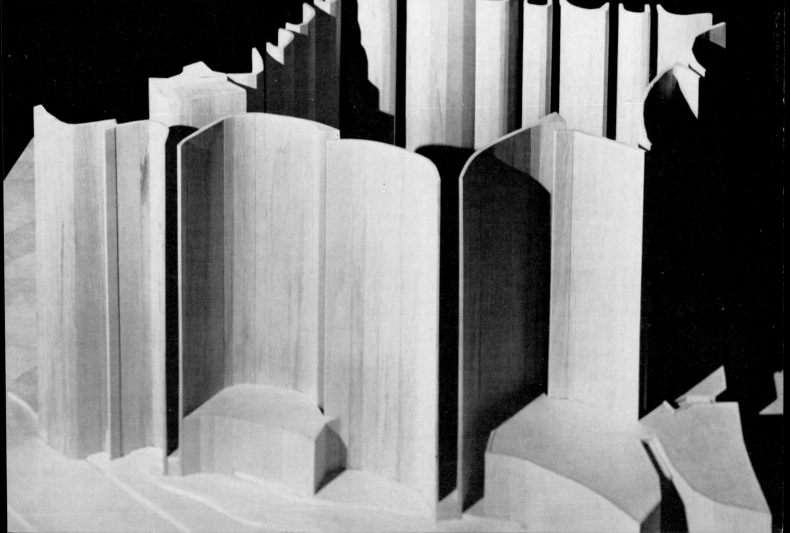

SWEDEN

Contributing Editor

Office of **Ralph Erskine**

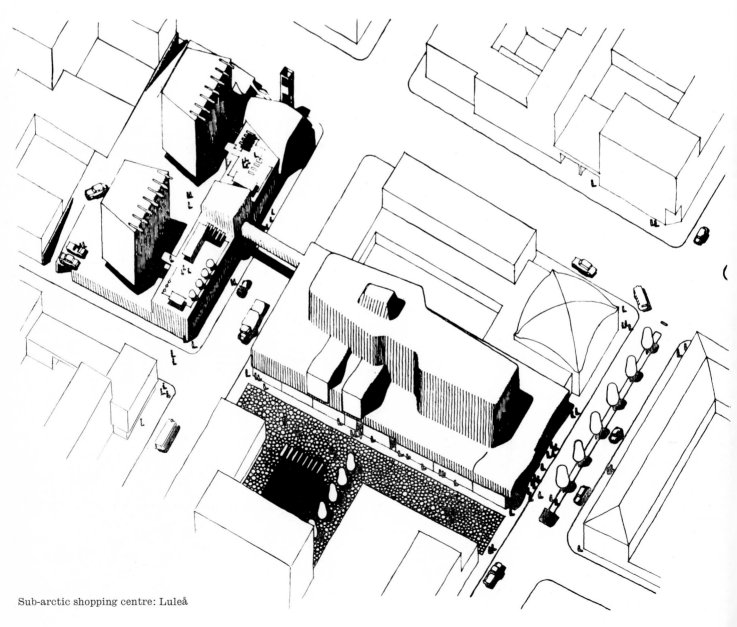

Sub-arctic shopping centre: Luleå

SUB-ARCTIC SHOPPING CENTRE: LULEÅ

Architect

Ralph Erskine

There are essential differences between the Luleå centre and its American equivalent. These are partly due to the specific character of the Swedish community and country. The most important points perhaps are that the building is placed in the centre of an existing community with the avowed intention of making it the heart of the town centre and of avoiding the destructive 'centrifugal' effect of certain suburban centres, and that it is consciously designed to meet the requirements of a 'sub-arctic' climate. Special problems also arose in that the scheme started as a small shop building but, during the designing and even construction periods, developed by stages to a building of four times the original size.

The Organization

The organization of the centre was built up by O. F. Sjöström, director, E. Lindberg, engineer, and S. Drape, economist. It consists of a central firm which rents shops to private shopkeepers, assists them with sales and purchasing advice and with window dressing and decoration (through the medium of a decoration studio), and handles joint promotion projects: fairs and festivities, advertising, distribution of brochures, purchaser information, mail order selling, and shopping tours for people coming from the whole of northern Sweden.

The Architectural Conception

This was developed some years earlier in a project designed by this architect's office for the city fathers of Kiruna, a town in the mountains well north of the polar circle. This 'sub-arctic centre' included dwellings: shops, restaurants and even a glazed nursery garden, grouped round a system of covered and heated streets and squares. The same principle was applied to the Luleå centre. As in the arcaded and mat-hung streets of tropical countries, climatic protection is extended outside the building, and includes the public streets and meeting places. Since, however, it is cold air, heat loss and snow and ice which have to be met, and not sun radiation, the open structures of the hot climates must here be exchanged for compact, well insulated buildings with a protective skin covering the whole structure and with moderate window areas where glass is not essential. These principles can of course be applied to all architecture in cold climates, and in larger units of city-centre type can become a roofed unit covering several blocks, with covered connections to secondary units.

The Application to Luleå

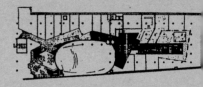

The Luleå project confines itself to the shopping building but with the aim of making it the real town centre. It has been placed in the junction of Luleå's two main shopping streets near the post office and other public buildings. It has also been given amusement and cultural functions as well as the purely commercial ones in order to make the building attractive for daily and evening shopping rounds, and provide entertainment for long-distance visitors from the interior of the Swedish north after shopping hours. The project consists of two interconnected buildings: one containing the majority of the shops, a cinema, restaurants, cafés, and a hotel; the other providing service facilities—loading bays, storage space, parking and garage space—and an amusement and exhibition area. The shop building is largely complete and is already in use; the service building is under construction.

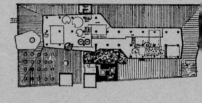

The streets of the city are drawn into the buildings through a warm air curtain, and continue as a system of 'lanes' and 'squares' with varying character, selling partly direct to the public through opened fronts: cafés and restaurants with 'outside' tables on the lanes, a cinema opening from the main square, a 'roof terrace' with service shops, beauty parlours and so on — all the life of a city centre. Dances and religious meetings, fashion parades, sales drives and art exhibitions follow one another in the main square; and there the people of Luleå meet one another, talk, and drink coffee. There is no doubt that this has already, after a few months, become the central square of Luleå, offering possibilities in its artificial climate for a social life which has hitherto been impossible during the long dark winter in the north, and barely possible in its often chilly summer.

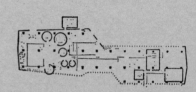

The plan has been given considerable variation so that, whilst admittedly the new visitor does not immediately appreciate the whole disposition, the constant visitor can always find a certain variation and intimacy.

The different streets are given varying character, and each square has a typical form, material and function in order to give visual impressions which assist orientation within the building, and in order to attract the public to all parts of it. The stiffening screens have a sculptural form; thereby forming orientation points.

It is important to remember that this building serves a rather small provincial town, and that purchasers here visit the building constantly and soon get to know it — a contrast to the multiple stores of a city with their anonymous public.

Construction and Materials

Durable materials — aluminium and glass — have been chosen for the covering which forms the protective 'hood' over the whole organism. Windows with threefold glass are moderate in size to reduce heat losses, but allow the low northern sun to reach far into the building. There are, however, large windows at street level and at the main entrance which permit contact between the street and the interior, provide show space, and allow light from the building to stream out over the surrounding streets.

The interior streets are characterized by simple, warm, north Swedish materials, and a mundane city atmosphere has been avoided. The structure is of exposed concrete, enclosing walls of rough boards from the surrounding forests; and floors of concrete slabs with a surface of granite shingle are the same as those which are laid on the exterior pavements around the building. Shopfronts vary from alley to alley and are in stained or painted wood or black steel.

Where suitable, shopfronts can be opened with sliding doors, or with shutters as in medieval times, to allow shopkeepers to offer their goods directly to people passing by. The intention is that the simple materials should give a feeling of public space to the circulation system of the building, and should make the public feel at ease, letting them enter the building without feeling obligated to buy. At the same time the building's function of housing a voluntary association of free shopkeepers under a common roof is emphasized.

In order to stress further and 'protect' the individual shop in this collective unit, fronts are varied, and many are not of extreme 'open front' type.

It is hoped that neon, posters and other natural decorative elements of commercial life will form the main decoration of the public space.

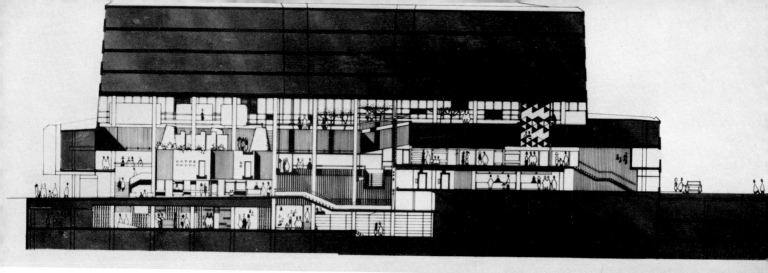

Section through streets, lanes and squares

Right The sculptural form of stiffening screens in exposed concrete creates orientation points in the internal streets.

Exterior at night

Photo: Sundahl

The cinema, which is also a concert, lecture and demonstration hall is built into the basement of the shopping centre at Luleå, and has its entrance from the 'central' square. The conception of the theatre is that of a 'light play' room from which the visual remnants of the conventional theatre have been excluded. It is constructed as a shell of sprayed concrete hung within the main structure of the building, and formed as a cyclorama which encloses the whole of the audience. Against the inner side of the shell, light, film and sound effects are thrown from a projection room which is suspended within the auditorium. From this room, and from two smaller projector groups near the stage, emanates the main lighting of the theatre. This lighting can be varied in colour, form and atmosphere to suit the

Free-form of exposed concrete staircases

Shop interior: an extension of the street

Dimly lit ambulatory around the auditorium

performance, and fades as the rays that carry the film, or the spotlights that illuminate the stage, direct the action to the far end of the room. The original intention was to treat the end wall as a screen, but the varied dimensions of films and the need for masking made an opening and a traditional film screen necessary. This opening is cut through the shell and has no surrounding frame. A curtain of the same almost white colour as the walls is hung as near the wall surface as possible and the screen is mounted behind this. The acoustic control of the interior is achieved almost entirely by its form, which is designed to reflect without echo. The acoustic qualities are excellent for films, chamber music and speech; and the room has been chosen as the most suitable in Luleå for radio programmes.

Shopping street: concrete, rough timber and steel

Gallery links across double-height space

The projection room suspended within the shell

GADELIUS HOUSE: LINDINGO

Architect

Ralph Erskine

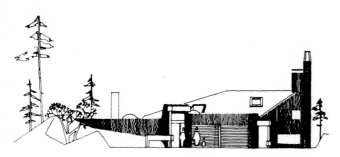 

This house represents a study of the function of the home; it also represents a stage in the search for an architecture which technically and aesthetically solves the specific problems of northern conditions. The enclosed form of the house is surrounded by free-standing elements consisting of the entrance shelters and the summer areas. The building is compact, and the moderate windows, designed to make the most of the views, are augmented by rooflights to light the interior. The house is designed to suit a site sloping steeply towards the Baltic coast, and to take advantage of the exceptionally fine view.

The Gadelius house has a free form, with its special scope for planning, adaptation to the profile of the ground, and the aesthetic experience of the shell's protective function.

The house is designed to form part of a group of three villas clustered round the edge of a small plateau between Lidingövägen and a steep slope down to Kyrkviken. The house is built into the terrain. Seen from the entrance-terrace and car-park, only the turf-covered roof and the three entrances are visible, these last being the car entrance (the most important in a suburban villa), the main entrance and the kitchen entrance. From these, steps lead down into the house, which widens out towards the summer terraces and follows the slope of the site towards the water. The roof is used as a garden, a flat area in the sloping terrain. A system of movable shelters has been arranged on the terraces to give shelter from the sun when necessary. The concrete supports for these shelters remain outside, and freeze up in the winter as a visible reminder of the summer.

The family has traditional connections with Japan, and has lived in Tokyo for several years. The house was designed both as a home and as a background for the client's duties as a host. This meant that apart from the communal rooms for the family, there should be secluded rooms for each individual. At the same time, the living-rooms should be capable of adaptation to suit groups of different sizes. This has been made possible by using a pillar construction to divide the living area into three, each part dominated by a different element: a window, a fireplace, and film and TV equipment. The dining area is also planned for flexibility by using a system of sliding doors. The childrens' rooms are near the kitchen, with a hobby-room below, and a neighbouring room for general purposes. The secluded room for the parents on the floor above is grouped with the mother's sewing-room and the father's study.

The house is built of concrete with internal insulation, and the interior generally is painted white. Externally, the concrete was left with the surface texture obtained from good formwork. The concrete is untreated, and where the house rises straight from the rock, house and rock sit together in harmony.

Photo: Ralph Erskine

Photo: Ralph Erskine

Above Entrance terrace

Right View from the garden

Garden view: winter

Garden entrance

Outdoor summer garden

Photo: Mats Linden

Softly top-lit spaces linked in a
continuous interior.

Free-standing structural elements
define functional areas in the open-
space plan. One area flows into
another, the whole interior a
setting for the Japanese art
collection.

Photo: Mats Linden

NORWAY

Contributing Editor

John Lloyd

The Cinderella of Scandinavia

Architecture and the arts have to struggle for recognition in Norway. This is due to a variety of reasons; some, such as the physical environment, are permanent, and others, such as the social-historical situation, are more transitory. In recent years this latter category has shown a distinct improvement and most of the work discussed here has come about because of this change in public opinion. It is essential to understand the peculiar nature of Norway's problems in order to appreciate the difficulties facing an architect and the reason why Norway has been the Cinderella of Scandinavia.

Theoretically Norway is an impossible political unit, as the country is extremely spread out with tortuous communications and a near subarctic climate. Very little of the country is habitable, not much more is productive and the result is the lowest population density of any political unit in Europe. Norway has always been a poor country, ruled for centuries by Denmark or Sweden. There has, therefore, never been any surplus within the community or a native ruling class, thus indigenous culture could only struggle to survive and never hope to develop. When, in 1905, Norway became a sovereign state she was also in many ways a pioneer land, building from scratch. Nonetheless, by the immediate prewar years the architectural situation was very promising and there had appeared an architect of ability, Ove Bang. During the war all this changed, Bang died, the architectural profession was isolated and introvert, and there was extensive destruction. The coastal towns, the districts around Narvik and the northernmost area were burnt down during the invasion and in the final phase of the war. To survive and have any chance of reconstructing the economy of the country it was absolutely necessary to re-house the population. This had to be done with whatever means and resources the country had. The effort overstrained the national economy. All building had to be spartan, and aesthetic considerations

SCANDINAVIAN PAVILION, VENICE
Arch: Sverre Fehn

219

SCHOOL, ASKER *Arch:* Geir Grung

were looked upon as non-essential luxuries. Following hard after this
emergency action came a large programme of domestic building financed
by the state and local authorities, but both the attitude and techniques
of the preceeding period were retained. It has taken fifteen years for
public opinion to awaken to the visual slums that these attitudes produced. This is due to two causes. First, Norway has practically no urban
tradition; virtually everyone is a first generation town dweller. Secondly,
the architectural profession in the post-war period was befogged and
without any clear leader or direction. It was only when the new generation, dissatisfied with this situation, was forced, with the help of a few
older men, to define a new field of action, that any progress could be made.
One can begin to talk of a broad front instead of pioneer groups. Altogether there seem to be certain general traits emerging which can be
characterized as a Norwegian style. There is the use of robust forms,
which can be seen in the best work throughout Norway's history, and
which is reappearing today. Notice, for example, the way in which roofs
are handled. There is the rough use of detailing and materials. One does
not see the refined handling of timber that one expects from Denmark,
but it is used in a mass, often emphasized by the use of black or brown
staining. This is expressive of a general preference for the direct use of
materials; the New Brutalists' programme has been the normal tradition
here and is continued today. Materials are understood much better and
valued more than is usual outside Scandinavia. This is one of the reasons
for the very high level of design in Scandinavian craftwork.
Building is still predominantly a craft affair in timber, concrete and
brick. Although timber framing has developed there has been no fundamental change in techniques; for instance, there are practically no
examples of membrane or shell construction. In the same way prefabrication and the industrialization of the building trade are very little prac-
tised. All this is mainly due to the low concentration of population and
difficult transportation. Transport costs usually prohibit the use of prefabrication and the small local contractors who are the main producers
cannot manage advanced techniques. The situation is slightly better in

MUSEUM, MAIHAUGEN, LILLEHAMMER *Archs:* Geir Grung and Sverre Fehn

the larger towns, but Norway has not the industrial breadth or capacity to support new materials and the market is not large enough to justify full industrialization.

While there is more organization and order even amongst those influenced by Knutsen one cannot yet talk of structural clarity apart from exceptional cases. It is perhaps because timber is the commonest material that one has not seen its structural possibilities clearly expressed. On the other hand Knutsen's feeling for the site has made everyone more conscious of the landscape. But his submission to the nature of a site can be misunderstood and used as an excuse for ignoring the site. One tends to see objects placed in the landscape as if it hardly existed, or occasionally an attempt has been made to obliterate the site altogether. The Norwegian landscape is not an easy one but it can be a constant source of inspiration. However, Norwegians have not yet come to terms with their untamed environment, and one is aware of a pioneer attitude. There is rarely any fine play between building and landscape; the architecture stops at the house and the landscape architect plays no part. The problem for the architect is to place an object in the landscape; it has been up to now impossible to find a successful example of the use of the milieu. Town planning is still thought of largely as a matter of zoning and traffic network. The problem of milieu has engaged many of the architects mentioned in this article together with a number of others for some time, but it is only now that any results are apparent. There are several modest attempts under construction, but no one has yet had the opportunity of a full scale project, and nothing is sufficiently advanced to publish. In the school in Oslo the students have just completed a study of a new town for 100,000 people which shows clearly that they are no longer concerned solely with the object in isolation but with the collective creation of an environment. Since this middle-range problem is being treated by an increasing number of architects competently and interestingly, there is every hope that Norway will now make good its lack of an urban tradition.

John Lloyd

221

National Romanticism

Photo: Teigens

In common with the rest of Scandinavia, Norway went through a period of national romanticism with Magnus Paulsen as its most powerful exponent. The elements of his architecture were the motifs taken from the old farm buildings, and these were used in a masterly fashion. Knut Knutsen, together with many other architects, was attracted by this work but he searched for a deeper meaning; for the essence of a regional architecture. He thus represented an aspect of a revived national romanticism, and for many in Norway this evoked an instinctive and sympathetic response, so that romanticism underwent sufficient metamorphosis to be a fruitful source of inspiration. He believed that nature must be preserved against human activity which would only result in its destruction. Therefore one must camouflage a building's form by use of irregular and small scale massing; materials must be 'natural' and colour only used for the same general purpose. These two basic trends — the search for a historical basis for a regional architecture and a desire to preserve the untouched landscape — reinforce one another and are understandable seen against the mainly rural conditions. Knutsen had a deep feeling for romanticism and the individual, as against classicism and an authoritarian society. His work clearly showed the influence of Frank Lloyd Wright and Alvar Aalto, but his point of

HOUSE, HØVIK, OSLO
Arch: Knut Knutsen

SOCIAL RESEARCH INSTITUTE, OSLO *Archs:* Lambertz-Nilssen and Trond Birger Eliassen (exterior and interior)

Photo: Bjørn Winsnes

Photo: Bjørn Winsnes

HOUSE, ULVØEN, OSLO
Arch: Knut Knutsen

HOUSE, MOELV
Arch: Are Vesterlid

Photo: Teigens

view was quite out of sympathy with the creation of an urban environment and was restricted in the use of new materials and techniques. Thus, while his work has had the strongest aesthetic influence on post-war Norwegian architecture, it is liable to make future developments more difficult, as it is exactly within the fields of town planning and new building techniques that we need to concentrate attention. Knutsen has been on the staff of the School of Architecture in Oslo since the war and has had a large influence on the students. It is from the graduates of this school that we can best judge his ideas. The most successful in this idiom is Are Vesterlid, in whose work one sees the same great care for the site, the same use of irregular form and handling of materials but in addition an interesting flow of space and a clearer use of structure. Trond Eliassen, Birger Lambertz-Nilssen and Per Cappelen are also consciously influenced by Knutsen, but they tend to organize form more clearly, and where they tackle a building in an urban environment they often organize to such a degree as to lose the typical visual appearance of the group's style. One sees how the handling of materials is at its best when most rustic, and occasionally the difficulty of using irregular forms becomes apparent.

Experimental room in timber
Archs: Per Cappelen and Østgaard

Photo: Teigens

HOUSE, LIER   *Arch:* Håkon Mjelva

SCHOOL, VETRE, ASKER   *Arch:* Geir Grung

Photo: Bjørn Winsnes

The second group to appear was the opposite of the first in almost every respect. It was smaller and its work has not led to such a uniform style.

Superficially it does not appear to have had such an immediate influence as the first. Another member of the staff of the school in Oslo was Arne Korsmo; he acted as a catalyst to this group, which did not accept the search for a Norwegian style as an answer to post-war architectural problems. Korsmo's role has been to put ideas in circulation rather than to lead by example. The group has drawn on many sources for its philosophy; they were also the most active members of post-war Norwegian C.I.A.M., and one of the group, Geir Grung, has continued as a member of Team 10. This group demanded a much stricter intellectual basis for architecture and as students were chiefly influenced by Bauhaus, C.I.A.M., Mies, and traditional Japanese architecture. Nowadays there would be nothing exceptional in this, but in these circumstances it was quite revolutionary and the results have been more obvious because of the group's isolation and general opposition to local developments. It functioned as a team called A.5 up to 1954 but has since split up. It is, however, interesting to note certain common traits. Sverre Fehn, Håkon Mjelva, and Christian Norberg-Skulz have all been teachers of design at the Oslo school, and together with Grung they have all been interested in advancing building technique and solving town-planning problems.

Since 1954 the group has developed in different directions. Norberg-Skulz has become an architectural historian; Grung has studied and produced system buildings; Mjelva has been engaged in town planning, and Fehn has been preoccupied with problems of pure form. But these special interests are questions of degree within a broad activity as architects. The group is therefore equipped to tackle the most acute architectural problems today and will probably do this in a convincing aesthetic way.

Group A5, C.I.A.M. and Team 10

HOUSE, OSLO
Archs: Arne Korsmo and Christian Norberg-Skulz

SCANDINAVIAN PAVILION, VENICE   *Arch:* Sverre Fehn

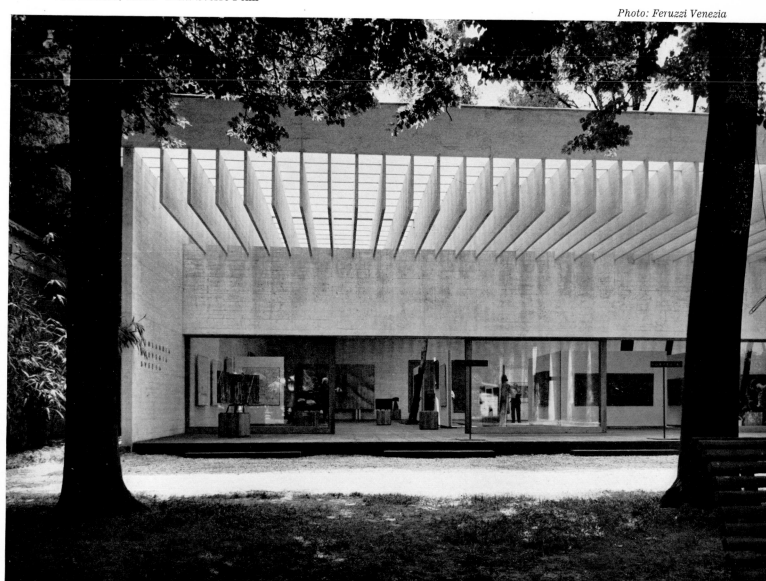

Photo: Teigens

TOWN HALL, ASKER *Archs:* K. Lund and N. Slaato

The Craftsmen

TELEGRAPH OFFICES, OSLO *Arch:* Nils Holter

Photo: Teigens

A third group also exists, mainly of older generation architects, and this is led by Nils Holter. These are the non-dogmatic, sober and competent craftsmen. Holter's work has always shown great attention to workmanship and detailing; his Broadcasting House, built in the thirties, has matured exceptionally well and the Telegraph House just finished is the best office block in Oslo to date. What makes the situation optimistic is that there have appeared in the last few years a number of younger architects producing this quality of work. It is quite natural that it has taken longer for these architects to appear, and it is interesting to see the influence on them of both the previous groups.

Photo: Bjørn Winsnes

HOUSE, OSLO *Arch:* T. Jønn

Photo: Bjørn Winsnes

SCHOLARSHIP CENTRE, VOKSENASEN, OSLO
Archs: H. Larsen, T. Thorstensen and Sundt Hansen

Photo: Bjørn Winsnes

GREAT BRITAIN

Contributing Editor

John Donat

A Dying Culture
and a Half-baked Architecture

Our architecture is US. If we hate it that is because we hate ourselves.
A great culture — complete, integrated and consistent — will produce a great architecture of its own kind. . . . A lousy culture — fragmented, decadent, dying or amorphous — produces a lousy architecture.
Architecture is a mirror of its age all right, but real architecture is also as cruel as a mirror. And our age, of course, has not got a very pretty face.
So, meanwhile, we must do the best we can with what we have got — a dying culture and a half-baked architecture.[1]

The Welfare State begs the question. Its achievement in schools, housing and town planning (doubts stirring in this sphere) is the envy of the world. But it is a weak protagonist confronted with the inexorable pressures of commercial exploitation, the land racket and property speculation. It has signally failed to resolve the crucial challenge to democratic society — planning for the benefit of the community *versus* freedom for the individual. This is not, perhaps, surprising — we instinctively distrust plans, we have not much faith in the planners. Meanwhile our cities are gradually being destroyed as places worth living and working in, and the green and pleasant land is being over-run by 50,000,000 semi-detached, individual freedoms.

The architect is pretty helpless. He can't opt out. He can't be a Rip van Winkle and sleep peacefully until a ready-made integrated society is clamouring for his indispensable talents. His only alternative is to act in isolation and work out his own private destiny on unrelated fragments of the environment. His architecture becomes more and more introverted and pursues its own obscure aims out of touch with the sympathy and understanding of the people it is for.

If the hard cold wind of truth, the stars and the depths of the sea, is to be our religion, as well it might be, then it must be an inspiration to a whole society. It must be understood, not hated, by the common man.
If our universities can also become — like those of the middle ages — repositories of Truth, then the universities may just possibly become the core around which life can once again become a real and integrated culture. They may also produce a real architecture. That, indeed, is the only grain of hope in the whole story.[1]

The younger architects, the *pacemakers*, may play a significant role in the long overdue expansion programme for the universities. Two buildings are presented here. Neither is a complete university; each in isolation is symptomatic of the current dilemma. One, in a provincial industrial city, accepts the university as a prelude to industry and clothes it in an appropriately industrial aesthetic. The other, in a medieval university town, re-interprets traditional university life in a unique if not entirely original form. Neither could possibly claim to be an integrated statement about an integrated culture: each is doing its best with what we have got.

ENGINEERING FACULTY, LEICESTER
Archs: Stirling and Gowan

[1] Fragments from *Architectural Horizons* by Robert Furneaux Jordan, Twentieth Century, Summer 1962

ENGINEERING FACULTY, LEICESTER

Architects

James Stirling and James Gowan

Like all the *pacemakers* Stirling and Gowan have been slavishly imitated: their ideas have spawned a whole family of clichés all over the country — the superficial form inevitably mistaken for the substance. With their early buildings they were in the van of the rough-edge cavemen — raw concrete, rough brickwork carved into heavyweight patterns, and medleys of monopitch roofs. Now they have left all the nostalgic rural artlessness behind and have designed their first *real* building, hard-edged and crackling.

It divides sharply into two: on the south are teaching laboratories sheathed in translucent white glass; on the north is a cluster of towers for administration, circulation and research, with a large and a small lecture theatre below. The whole tower-cluster is clad in matched brick and tile (walls, floors, even ceilings).

When the architects describe the building, they conceal far more than they reveal, reducing the process of design to a neat package of functional needs and logical solutions. One longs to hear the *real* reasons, to learn something about the undefined territory between logic and creativity, between science and art. Why should the creative act — the built dream — be so sinful and embarrassing?

It took more than the need for oblique north light to create that necklace of glittering white diamonds; more than the need for a balanced structure to thrust the lecture halls' red wedges into the sky; more than the client's distaste for concrete to wrap every surface in skin-tight brick and tile; more than a cramped site to thrust out the cantilevered jaws that gobble up machinery from below; more than the angle of the boundary to chamfer off all the tower-cluster corners . . . and in this building it is the *more* that matters. The functions have been absorbed and fulfilled, but they burst out in a superbly disciplined riot of form that owes as much to the heart as to the mind. Inside, the riot is not so disciplined, the form less precise, the magic has lost something of its lustre. Laboratories filled with complex machinery are visually chaotic at the best of times. It is inevitable that the wide open interiors, wrapped in a web of structure and services, should tell a very different story to the crisp kaleidoscope of mirrors outside. At least, the uncompromising workshop atmosphere stands more chance of survival than the genteel tidiness so many architects attempt to impose on scientists. Ultimately it is for them to judge. Will they turn their industrial jewel into just another shed?

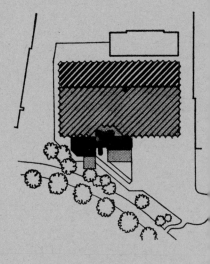

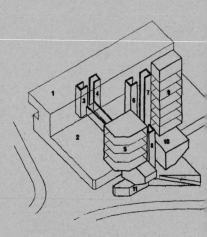

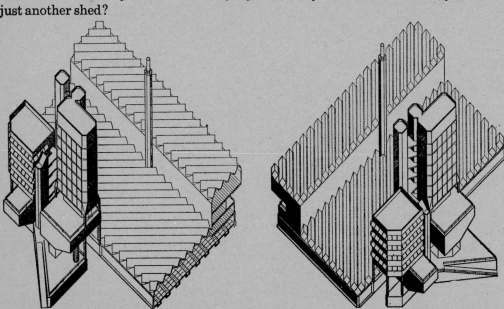

ISOMETRIC KEY
1 Teaching laboratories
2 Heavy laboratories
3 Stairs
4 Lifts
5 Research laboratories
6 Stairs
7 Lifts
8 Stairs
9 Administration
10 Lecture theatre
11 Lecture theatre

Above Tower cluster from park

Above right Research tower projecting windows

Right Ensemble

Below Teaching laboratories exterior

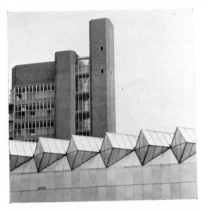

Photos: John Donat

Above Tile-clad circulation spaces

Right Large lecture theatre interior
and lecture theatres exterior

Below Teaching laboratories

HALL OF RESIDENCE, CAMBRIDGE

Architect

Sir Leslie Martin in association with Colin St John Wilson

Caius is the illegitimate offspring of a shotgun marriage between Le Corbusier and Alvar Aalto. Built on a suburban site remote from the parent college, it has been designed to be inward looking and self-contained. As a result, the section of La Tourette has been turned inside-out so that the undergraduates face into the central space and not away from it, and the relaxed informality of Säynätsalo has been squared-off to concentrate the self-contained image. But even though the rough passion of Corbusier has been softened and the subtle nature of Aalto hardened, the building does have an authority of its own.

The stepped section wrapped around a central court is based on a principle of growth that can be extended consistently in the future by the addition of a second related court. Inside, the planning is based on the traditional arrangement of study-bedrooms identified in small groups around staircases opening off the cloister. In this case the cloister has become a broad ambulatory around the outside perimeter of the raised ground floor, and each staircase is skilfully integrated with the overhanging step-out section and richly modelled on the exterior. One result of this system is that all the rooms open out on to wide communal terraces at the very point where one expects to reach privacy. It may be impossible to work when the terraces are littered with deck chairs, beer bottles and record players, but on the other hand, if you can't make friends in this building you are unlikely to make them anywhere. There is a strong reaction within the universities against the compartmenting of undergraduates into blinkered specializations and this building intentionally encourages social contact.

The main communal rooms are at ground floor level; the common rooms open on to the garden and the breakfast room impinges on the central court as a stunted brick pyramid of roof-lights.

Materials are restricted to a spartan minimum: brick structure and paving, with windows and doors in varnished douglas fir. These simple materials have been handled brilliantly to emphasize the powerful sculptural nature of plan and section. The result is a tough building, bound by its nature to impose its will. Walking around and through it you really feel in the presence of something, a quality not many modern buildings can claim. Even so, the medieval undertones are disturbing, the rigorous formality has a dogmatic ring. One wonders if the undergraduates are contained within those four crisp corners for their own benefit or for the sake of the architecture.

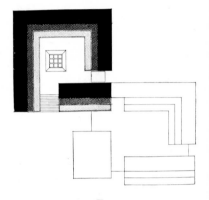

GONVILLE AND CAIUS BLOCK PLAN

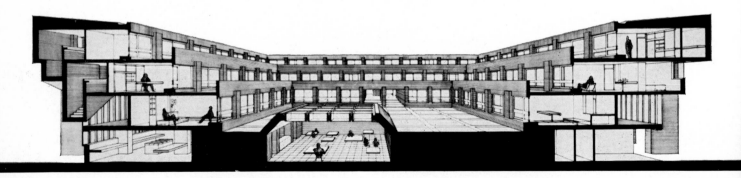

Photos: John Donat

Left Breakfast room roof-lights

Below Steps to court from garden

Above Brickwork detailing

Left Main entrance canopy

Photos: John Donat

Study-bedroom

Sliding window to open terrace

Ground floor ambulatory

Common room interior

COMPUTER OFFICES, WORCESTER

Architects

Howell, Killick, Partridge and Amis

This building is a deliberate break away from flat-faced curtain walling. Brick, glass and matt-black aluminium play the modelling game according to their own rules; the brick as a sharply etched composition of irregular, vertical solids and voids, the glass and aluminium as a wrap-around profile playing in-and-out with the structural frame. High-level ventilating hoppers are deeply recessed and shaded by the projecting slabs, aluminium clad undercill panels project beyond the frame to enable the service pipes to travel horizontally outside the structure, and a median plane is established by the fixed main glazing.

The planning is straightforward and very largely determined by the limitations of a strait-jacket site restricted by roads on three sides and by an existing brick office building on the fourth to which two connections with the new accommodation were required. These two links enclose a small patio-garden and slide between the three main components of the plan: on the north, the computer room with accurately controlled humidity and temperature; in the centre, a block of offices designed for flexibility of layout with good sound insulation; and on the south, a brick ancillary block whose monumental form seems rather inappropriate to the functions it serves (staircases, lavatories and tea kitchens). The junctions between the three main elements are treated with religious deference as points of articulation.

The choice of materials and colours has been carefully controlled and kept to a minimum. Apart from using a similar brick in sympathy with the existing office building (which deserves no sympathy at all), the brick, glass and metal are explored in their own right in the adventure of the search for form. Each has a job to do, must be seen to do it and must assume a form appropriate to the role it plays in relation to the total idea. The adventure is restrained and sophisticated, finding genuine delight in the rules of its own game; the turning of a corner, the meeting of surfaces and the connection of one part with another.

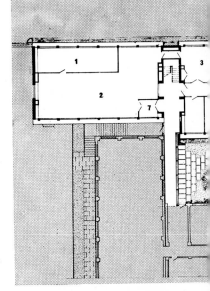

PLAN KEY
1 Tape room   6 Library
2 Computer room 7 Airlock
3 Workshop   8 Offices
4 Tabulator room 9 Typists
5 Punching room 10 Patio garden
                  11 Pool

Photos: John Donat

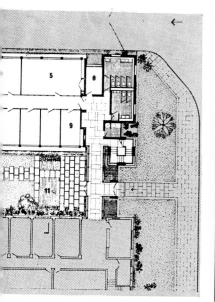

Above Computer room north

Above right Courtyard link to new building

Below right Staircase link between computer room (right) and offices

Photos: John Donat

COMPUTER OFFICES: INTERIORS   *Above* Clerestory lit corridor

Below left Typical office corner detail

Below right Main staircase

TELEVISION CENTRE, DUBLIN

EIRE

Architect

Michael Scott

A television centre is a factory for the production of programmes. The relationship between scene-docks, studios, dressing rooms, production control, technical ancillaries and administration is crucial to efficient production and has to be based on a principle of flexibility and growth to allow for the prodigious expansion rate of television. In this case, although the studios were only designed for seven hours live transmission a week, they are already turning out nearly three times as much.

The architect has organized the highly complex technical functions in a brilliant system of vertical and horizontal layers. All heavy factory work (studios, scenery, heavy camera equipment) forms a base layer at ground floor level serviced direct from outside beneath a covered colonnade that encircles the whole perimeter. Production control, technical ancillaries and administration comprise the second vertical layer at first floor level and are arranged in a secondary system of horizontal layers to allow each department to expand independently. The main studios (built of isolated mass concrete for effective sound insulation) rise up through the first floor and project through the roof in a third vertical layer which contains the complicated lighting control grids and air-conditioning plant.

The simplicity of the final result, an elegant rectangle standing in a large field, belies the complexity within, but the layer system works. It also succeeds as an interpretation of the Miesian tradition. The modular system is consistent and clear, the materials used are few and good, though by no means luxurious. The whole design, inside and out, is elegant, underplayed and cool. It all seems incredibly un-Irish. Perhaps such a perfect mirror of the efficient technical organization of television can hardly be expected at the same time to reflect the human idiosyncrasies, the incorrigible charm of the people it was built for, and for whom it must be an inscrutable enigma.

Photo: John Donat

Left and above Elliptical stair to first floor reception area

Below Entrance elevation

Above Reception area
Above right Typical corridor

Photos: John Donat

Right Main studio
Below Perimeter colonnade

CANADA

Contributing Editor

Anthony Jackson

Photo: Clive H. Clark

Housing A Middle Class Nation

America is a continent of myths: myths of cowboys and indians; myths of free enterprise. While fishing, farming, coal-mining and transportation get massive support from central government funds, everyone knows that he must stand on his own two feet. 'Work not dole', chanted the lower middle class during the depression. Europeans might have called them the working class but no such thing exists in North America. So, even when in 1934 about 12,000,000 Americans were out of work, the unions did not become political. They only wanted the capitalists to start making money again so that they could go back to having their share of it. Of course, in Canada the depression was not so bad. If you are destitute anyway, what is a depression? After all, everyone knows it cannot last. With 3,500,000 square miles and a population of only 16,000,000 Canada's needs are obvious. All we have to do is open up the land and build up our industry. As Herbert Hoover once said: 'The business of America is business'. And that goes for here too.

Only, somehow, we are not the same. America used to be called America until Canada got out of the doldrums in the war re-armament programme. Now we call that place the United States and the two of us North America. And we have differences. The United States never did get a real socialist party, but we have the NDP. And while they have one of the finest welfare states, we still go along with free enterprise. Yes, their captains of industry have become public servants. When the Americans talk about free enterprise they mean government-approved corporation trusts. We mean the real thing. You and I might be just wage earners today, but tomorrow, with a bit of hard work, we too can have a Cadillac and culture. That is the funny thing. We still have a pioneering economy but borrow our 'up-to-the-minute mores' from across the border.

Where does all this lead? North America builds for the middle class. The rich look after themselves; the poor are in need of social welfare, but everyone knows that they would not be poor if they did not have some moral or mental deficiency. So they are put in ghettoes where they can be cared for and, when they are cured and can pay the rent, they are put outside — approved citizens; though by some overwhelming logic of society you can earn too little to be allowed inside in the first place. Free enterprise builds for the middle class. And does it build! Sub-divisions sprawl around our cities, sub-divisions of little bungalows, everyman's broadacre city. Put up for the quickest financial return and guaranteed to sell by our housing mortgage policy. Our sub-divisions are not planned by designers but by surveyors marking out lots. No wonder that when someone actually tries we overwhelm him with praise, whatever the result. Anything is better than nothing.

So, in North America, Radburn is a classic. Started just before the 1929 depression and never completed, it caused the bankruptcy of a public-spirited group that had hoped to build an American garden city. What remained? Instead of 25,000 people, 400 familes. Instead of a garden city, a garden suburb. No green belt, no offices, no

FLEMINGDON PARK, TORONTO
Arch: Irving Grossman

industry, no communal land ownership but a benevolent despotic management. It had a school, some stores and community rooms — and parks and pools and playgrounds. Why is it important? Because, for the first time, a neighbourhood was designed around a communal space so that people could walk out of their gardens, along a path, into a park. Automobiles, 21,000,000 of them in 1928, were fingered into service roads, across vehicular routes, underpasses and overpasses. The Radburn idea. The suburbs had been set in order, but they still remained the suburbs. To quote one of Radburn's planners: 'One can cross a couple of lawns and call out "Who's home?" ' Fulfilling the North American ideal, Radburn was for white, white-collar protestants.

A few years later, after the banks had gone bankrupt, the American government took a hand. Ignoring all the sacred myths, the Roosevelt administration set up in business themselves. The garden city became government policy. Greenbelt in Maryland, thirteen miles from the centre of Washington, was a re-settlement project for the unemployed. Throughout, the degree of co-operation was idyllically un-American. Even the shopping centre became a co-operative. Initially housing about 3,000 people, the crescent-shaped town is divided into superblocks. Inside, Radburn planning frees the pedestrian. The houses have semi-private gardens and the whole town is surrounded by a green belt. The people were mixed in District of Columbia proportions: thirty per cent Catholic, seven per cent Jewish, with professional, clerical and manual workers. But no jobs in the town; Greenbelt is a dormitory for Washington, and while the women gather in the community crescent heart, the men go off to the big city.

Architecturally of course, if architecture is only to do with building aesthetics, Radburn and Greenbelt are nothing to talk about; but look forward a few more years. After the re-settlement, administration was handed over to the Department of Agriculture to become part of the Farm Security Administration, Richard Neutra was given Channel Heights to design on the coast of the Pacific Ocean. The design of the units is certainly better — he got an AIA Honor Award for them. But what has happened to the community? Here there is no overall sense of purpose. The Radburn circulation device of pedestrian and service roads is used to create a suburban sprawl. Building design has replaced community design.

In the nineteen-twenties when there was going to be a bright new world, a group was formed by people like Clarence Stein and Henry Wright who had designed places like Chatham Village and Radburn, Alexander Bing who had built Radburn, and others like Lewis Mumford who were involved with questions of environment. During the new deal when men were brothers, they worked together for a better way of life. But when economy got going again, we were all just too busy making money to worry about such utopian problems. So, when anyone manages to produce a housing development that is only a bit worse than those built by our fathers, we are so astonished that we give them a medal.

In 1960 even the architectural profession became aware that housing might be of some concern to architects. The Canadian Institute set up a committee of inquiry. Overwhelmed by the belief that the architect is universal man, the architects went it alone. On the basis that an open (empty?) mind is all that is needed, the architects invited other specialists to give evidence before the committee. One social economist who declined this offer said later about their report: 'The fundamental realities of politics, of economics, of education, seem to have been overlooked, if not swept aside in a rush of artistic enthusiasm.' One of the questions the committee asked itself was: What sort of residential areas do we want to live in? The answer seems to be neighbourhoods where there are rich and poor, owners and tenants, old and young, apartments and houses, natives and foreigners, families and bachelors. In short: that every possible measure should be taken to encourage diversity among these new dwellings.

The following year the Central Mortgage and Housing Corporation, the government agency that largely financed the inquiry, sponsored an architectural competition for

FLEMINGDON PARK, TORONTO

FLEMINGDON PARK, TORONTO

the design of a model neighbourhood in Ottawa. The conditions set out a rigid middle-class occupancy for those with an income between $85 (£30) and $130 (£45) a week. The winning design carefully separated house owner from tenant, apartment from house. The fundamental realities overlooked by the committee of inquiry were set right by the facts of life.

Don Mills is another sort of garden city, planned by private developers in 1952 for a target population of 35,000. The town is divided into four by crossroads and further segmented by an inner and outer ring road. Inside the inner circle are the shopping centre, sports facilities, library and other community buildings. Here, too, are the office and apartment buildings. Each outer quadrant is a residential neighbourhood. At either end of the town is an industrial group located by railway lines which make an outer triangle defining the town shape. People actually live and work there. Don Mills is planned like a town but it is *inside* metropolitan Toronto. The people who live there could live somewhere else but they do not. They live in Don Mills inside a city of 1,500,000 people, with the city centre twenty-five minutes away by car and discouragingly difficult to get to by public transport. Presumably they are happy. In the winter they drive to their neighbours while the kids go tobogganing; in summer they lounge in bermuda shorts and drive out to the cottage at the weekend. In the evenings they go bowling. The teenagers date and play at sex until they get caught. The children ride around on the roads. Canadians like the good life.

Down in the city the lights sparkle, the young huddle around coffee bars which are springing up near the town-house neighbourhood of the rich; the streetcars clang past the store windows through the Italian slums, out of which the last generation of Jews have moved.

So what? Some people like to live in towns, some people like to live in suburbs. The people who live in towns like variety, the people who live in suburbs like conformity. Do not forget Canada has no social classes. The butcher's accent is the same as his doctor's. All that counts is how much you earn. So as our standard of living climbs our middle class gets ever larger. And middle-class people have middle-class values. They neither want to live in the centre of the city nor too far away from it, for in North America the city centre is the central business district. What they want are garden suburbs within commuting distance of city amenities. For after all, what is a city but a place to get out of?

Don Mills then is all right in principle if you don't want to alter the North American way of life. If you do, you should remember that the United States has the highest standard of living in the world and still can give away enough to keep the rest of us out of trouble. Canada has the second highest; or is it Sweden — though it can't be Sweden for, as Eisenhower said, a socialist country must be sick. Anyhow, it is obvious that free enterprise gives the people what they want, even if it has to spend billions of dollars to make them see what they want. The only thing wrong with Don Mills is that architecturally it is a mess. This may seem surprising considering that it was architecturally controlled, but contrast the elegant shopping centre designed by Canada's equivalent of SOM with the rambling shambles of the housing around. How the architect's heart bleeds! Oh to take those chaotic units, put them together and give them scale and rhythm, to take those eighteen-foot automobiles and get them lined up longest on the left shortest on the right, to do away with those cabbage patches and lay out a park worthy of royalty: to get some architectural order out of this human chaos.

Well, this is what Flemingdon Park is doing. Its town plan is not as good as Don Mills, but its housing is probably architecturally better than any recent housing on the North American continent. Is it better than Don Mills to live in? I do not know. I would not live in either. Both Grossman and myself live downtown.

Anthony Jackson

Photo: Clive H. Clark

FLEMINGDON PARK, TORONTO

Architect

Irving Grossman

What succeeds at Flemingdon Park is that the buildings are virile, varied, individual — humane (except for the apartment slabs which have simply been taken over direct from modern orthodoxy without re-analysis). The buildings are rhythms setting out paths of movement, on occasion defining broad spaces. The rhythm takes place against the sky. In the sub-areas planned by Grossman, where the car has been funnelled under the ground, a pedestrian community is established — neither urban nor suburban. The streets above the roads are on occasion doll's house in scale and rather like a stage set; the space behind the dwelling row spreads away, leaving the street isolated in its urbanity. Behind: the North American togetherness which eschews individual gardens and peers through the curtains of glass walls. Major and minor spaces collide at the building walls; collar and tie supplant jeans and sweat shirt — town and country. But town is only used by visitors and tradesmen when the car is in the basement and the country is just around the corner. So the street is primarily for ordering access, and the community remains middle-class Canadian with broad spaces to meander in. But where else can you find such space? To reach a downtown park you first have to survive the traffic. To reach a suburban park you have to drive there. At Flemingdon Park the park is outside your door. Who could ask for more? Perhaps it is not necessary to have a park outside *every* door, but if you do not have a private garden, and developers are convinced that we do not want gardens, then a park is really the next best thing. Community and identity; the suburbs have neither. Flemingdon Park is delineated by major traffic routes, including a parkway that takes you to the centre of Toronto at fifty miles an hour. It has offices and industry, but these are part of the metropolitan pattern. It has community facilities but, built by other architects, these are architecturally indifferent. It has a sense of time because Grossman develops with his designs. How do these estates grow old? Leasehold gives the developer a sense of responsibility but the community little chance of redeveloping itself. The architect usually adds his claim to eternity. But here the pattern is the diversity permitting change and idiosyncracy within its evolution. The architect leaves the site and the buildings take over. An environment has been established.

Anthony Jackson

Photo: Baltazar Korab

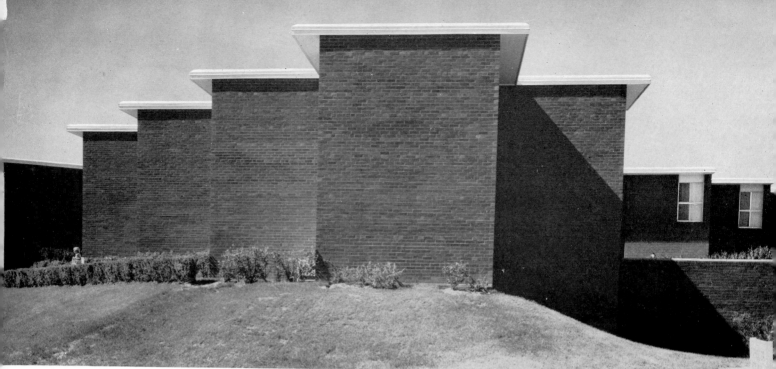

Photo : Clive H. Clark

I have always felt that the problems inherent in quantity, in numbers of dwellings, demand a non-art approach if such is possible in architecture. I would like to create an environment in mass housing, where the architect's hand is not apparent, yet it sings. The vital things are not the jewels but the overall feeling of well-being. Large-scale domestic architecture should be like good film music — you feel good in its presence, but when you leave you cannot really recall the exact images or details. I think at Flemingdon Park we have tried for the sculptured effects of in and out, up and down. One could accept a smooth, more formal approach — for a downtown site perhaps.

What these thoughts — human scale ... nature ... the machine — resulted in at Flemingdon, in part, was the idea of placing the car below the pedestrian street. A simple idea — the car moving and parking below, people living and walking above: both circulation routes tied to the dwelling units like an umbilical cord. This concept allowed and even established new forms and relationships, which at once made possible a number of developments:

Direct contact between car and dwelling Our comfort-seeking society demands the convenience of direct, under-cover access between house and car. The air-lock, a permanently ventilated and pressurized vestibule through which one has to pass between house and garage, ensured safety and was acceptable to the local building department.

Elimination of asphalt wastelands The concealed drives leading to cars parked underground avoided the acres of asphalt that high-density groupings usually demand. The site is now virtually left green, and the proper relationship of building to nature becomes much easier.

The intimate pedestrian walks These occur above the auto routes and lead to every front door. The space is defined, geared to the pedestrian, to the playing child and the strolling couple. Even the fountain can once more be revived.

The identity of dwelling Governed by the street cross-section and within its limitations, any kind of dwelling unit can be fixed to the circulation route. There is no need to think in terms of buildings, only party walls between which anything can happen. Identity of habitat is still possible.

Variation of form and space   As the vocabulary of unit types increases, to be freely disposed between party walls according to demand, orientation and other needs, so the form of the streets becomes varied and exciting. When the architectural firm of Klein & Sears, working on other Wehin projects, developed the principle of wedge-shaped plan forms that create a curving pattern when placed together, a further range of formal and spatial possibilities was uncovered. The street could now turn, form crescents or twist almost snake-like down and around the most unlikely sites. When we later evolved the zig-zag unit several more planning and formal implications were seen — windows that looked down the long view of the street instead of across, rear gardens with privacy arising from effect walls, the strong rhythm of shadows and projections from the broken façade. The scope is limitless. It is here that exploration can take place.

Photo: Clive H. Clark

High density — direct access   The compactness with which the linear growth of the street can be manipulated allows increased densities. Row houses, conventionally set at five to twelve units to the acre, are easily planned at eighteen to twenty-five units to the acre, with ample open space remaining. When one stacks row houses over each other in the form of terraced units, the densities rise again, approaching those of standard three-storey apartment buildings. On consideration, it seems that any such form of tiered dwelling, providing a private front door and a rear garden or roof terrace (not balcony), would be preferable for family living to any type of corridor apartment-accommodation. The privacy of these self-contained dwellings strikes a note of individuality that not even the luxurious apartment can offer, and the children remain close to the ground where they can move freely.

Irving Grossman

Photo: Baltazar Korab

Index

Architects and contributors

Buildings and projects